MATHS WITH MATHOMAT

A SERIES OF LESSON PLANS FOR YEARS 4 TO 9 AND BEYOND

Susie Groves and Peter Grover

Published by

Objective Learning Materials
A business of W & G Australia Pty. Ltd.
Unit 1, 7–9 Brough Street,
Springvale, Victoria, 3171
Phone: (03) 9796 1177
Fax: (03) 9796 1832
Website: www.mathomat.com.au

First Edition 1999
Reprinted 2008

ISBN 0-9586103-0-4

Designed and Typeset by
A Head in Graphics
Kilsyth, Victoria, 3137.

Artwork by
Commodore Press Pty Ltd
100 Beresford Road,
Lilydale, Victoria, 3140.
Website: www.commodore.com.au

Printed in Australia by
Commodore Press Pty Ltd
100 Beresford Road,
Lilydale, Victoria, 3140.
Copyright © Susie Groves and Peter Grover

This book is copyright. Apart from any fair dealings for purposes of private study, research, criticism or review, as permitted under the Copyright Act, no part may be reproduced, stored in a retrieval system or transmitted, in any form or by any means electronic, mechanical, photocopying, recording, or otherwise, without written permission. Inquiries should be made to the publisher.

Worksheet, handout and transparency masters are intended for reproduction in quantities sufficient for classroom use. Permission is hereby granted to the purchaser to produce each master in quantities suitable for non–commercial classroom use.

Contents

Foreword v

Acknowledgments vii

How to Use This book 1

Practical Tips 3

The Lessons

1   **Shape Up! Sort Me Out!** 5
    Familiarisation with MATHOMAT

2   **Tiles, Tiles and More Tiles** 11
    Patterns Using Transformations

3   **Don't Be Square!** 21
    Parallel Lines and Isometric Grids

4   **Bigger and Bigger** 31
    Enlarging Figures to Construct Polyhedra Nets

5   **This Looks Like That!** 39
    Investigating Symmetry

6   **The Area is Right!** 47
    Estimating and Measuring Areas

7   **Straight Line Curves** 57
    Constructing Envelopes of Curves

8   **Where Are We?** 65
    Maps, Bearings and Distances

9   **Round and Round the Circle** 79
    Rotational Symmetry

10 **Stars, Circles and Mystic Signs** 89
    Creating Patterns with Circles

11 **Unwrapping the Circle** 99
    Constructing the Sine Graph

Foreword

This series of lesson plans has been developed to give teachers of years 4 to 9 and beyond a glimpse of the tremendous potential for using the MATHOMAT as an aid in the teaching of mathematics.

Many of the ideas behind these lesson plans have come from Craig Young's instruction book which was written for the original MATHOMAT.

In this book, however, these and other ideas for using the MATHOMAT have been expanded to form comprehensive lesson plans which teachers can adapt for their own use.

Each lesson plan clearly identifies the purpose and mathematical content of the lesson and provides a list of materials required, an outline of the lesson and photocopy masters for any worksheets, handouts or transparencies required.

As indicated by the title of this book, *Maths With Mathomat: A Series of Lesson Plans for Years 4 to 9 and Beyond*, the lesson plans are aimed at a range of year levels—these are listed on the first page of each lesson. Typically a lesson might be designed for years 4 to 8 or years 5 to 9. Clearly teachers will need to adapt the lesson plans to suit the level of the students they teach.

Tables included in the book link the lessons to the outcomes in National and State mathematics curriculum documents—of necessity, these frequently cover a fairly wide range of levels.

Most of the lessons, if done in full, require more than 45 minutes, some substantially so. Teachers may wish to complete part of a lesson within a single session or plan to devote several sessions in order to complete the full lesson.

We hope you and your students enjoy using these lessons as much as we have enjoyed producing them!

Susie Groves and Peter Grover

Acknowledgments

We would like to thank the people who have helped us develop this book. Many teachers and students in primary and secondary schools participated in trials of the activities found in the lessons. Julie Ryan and Terry Beeby produced early drafts of some of the lessons and carried out evaluations as part of the project which resulted in this book.

M.C. Escher's illustrations in Lesson 2 have been reproduced with permission from Cordon Art B. V., Baarn, Holland.

The Senufo wooden mask, Ivory Coast/Mali/Upper Volta used in Lesson 5 on Transparency 5.1 has been reproduced from Williams, G. (1971), *African Designs From Traditional Sources*, Dover Pictorial Archive Series, with the permission of Dover Publications.

Copies of maps used in Lesson 8 were produced from *Melway Street Directory* Edition 26, with permission from Melway Publishing Pty Ltd, Melbourne, Australia.

Lori Head, graphic artist from A Head in Graphics, provided valuable technical advice and assistance. John Lawton, of W & G Australia, the publisher of this book and the producer of MATHOMAT, provided unfailing support and displayed extreme patience with the passing of deadlines for completion of the project.

How to Use This Book

The purpose of this book is to give teachers a glimpse of the tremendous potential of MATHOMAT as an aid in the teaching of mathematics. The target audience for this book is upper primary and junior secondary teachers, although some lessons, such as Lesson 11, Unwrapping the Circle, may be used with senior secondary students.

Most people tend to think of the MATHOMAT as a sophisticated drawing instrument which is particularly appropriate for the teaching of space. However the lessons in this book cover not only key concepts in space, but also other areas, such as measurement, trigonometry, algebra and number, and involve students in carrying out investigations and communicating their results.

Lesson structure

The title page of each lesson contains its name, the year levels for which the lesson is intended, a 'sub-title' for the lesson which indicates the content of the lesson and a brief summary, which expands on this sub-title in terms of the mathematical content of the lesson and what the teacher can expect students to do during the lesson.

The second page of each lesson lists the materials required for the lesson and provides a lesson summary.

The next section of each lesson provides background information for the teacher. Sometimes this information relates to the purpose and organisation of the lesson, while at other times it discusses the underlying mathematics involved.

These preliminary sections are followed by the Lesson Outline, which describes, in detail, each stage of the lesson.

Where appropriate, photocopy masters of worksheets, handouts and overhead transparencies are provided, together with references to other resources.

Adapting the lessons

Because of the wide range of year levels suggested for each lesson, teachers may need to adapt the content in order to tailor it specifically for their class.

Most of the lessons, if done in full, require more than 45 minutes—some a great deal more. Teachers may wish to complete part of a lesson within a single session or devote several sessions to complete the full lesson.

Classroom organisation

While all of the lessons can be conducted using whole class instruction, students working individually, and class discussion, it is often a great advantage to have students working collaboratively in groups to carry out the tasks. Organisationally, the time required for a lesson can be much less if students in a group share a task such as measuring areas of shapes. Educationally, when students work in groups on some of the tasks in these lessons, they are forced to come to grips with mathematical terminology, as well as to explain the reasons behind their solutions. An essential feature of most lessons is the class discussion, which should occur not only at the end of lessons, but also at various stages throughout the lesson.

Practical Tips

- Students may benefit from some drawing tips so that precision drawing skills are fostered during the activities.

- Encourage students to use a sharp pencil or a fine-point pen.

- Use unlined paper.

- As they trace the shape, students should gently press on template near the shape being drawn.

- In order to get sharp corners on traced shapes, students should make sure that they hold the pencil or pen upright and draw each line segment from corner to corner, rather than the whole shape with one sweep of the hand.

- In some lessons, pencils are preferable to pens as incorrect lines and construction lines which do not form part of the finished designs can be erased if necessary.

- When students are constructing three-dimensional models from card, they should always use a fine-point pen and the edge of the MATHOMAT to lightly score all fold lines. This is a very important step in constructing neat solids with sharp edges. However it takes practice to produce score lines which are sufficiently firm but which do not rip the card. Students should practise this on scrap pieces of card before scoring their nets. The fact that the resulting edges are marked in pen does not detract from the finished solid.

LESSON 1

Shape Up! Sort Me Out!

Years 4 to 8

Familiarisation with MATHOMAT

This lesson presents some activities for student exploration of the stencil shapes on the MATHOMAT. Students will become aware of the range of shapes available for tracing, as well as some possible classifications of these shapes.

In this lesson students will:

- classify and sort geometrical shapes;
- develop their knowledge of mathematical terminology; and
- identify properties of shapes.

Materials Required

For each student:

- a MATHOMAT;
- unlined paper (scrap paper will do);
- a fine-point pen or pencil;
- scissors (optional—see later sections for details); and
- a sheet of A4 paper to display their results (or, if students work in groups, one sheet of A3 card or paper per group to use as a poster).

Lesson Summary

- Introducing the MATHOMAT—free play;
- students group shapes according to categories of their choice;
- sharing and discussion;
- (optional extension) playing Guess My Family; and
- (further extension—if time is available) creating attractive designs with the MATHOMAT.

For the Teacher

The MATHOMAT template contains 40 stencils, as well as a protractor, various drawing guides and rulers.

The shapes include: triangles; rectangles; other quadrilaterals; a regular pentagon; regular hexagons; a regular octagon; circles; and ellipses.

Other drawing aids include: a sin/cos curve; parabolas; a circle centre finder; a protractor; parallel, perpendicular and isometric grid guides; a half regular dodecagon; and various rulers, including a number line and a radian scale.

The large number of features on the template may at first glance present a daunting (although exciting) array for the student. This lesson aims to familiarise students with the various shapes on the MATHOMAT in order to allow them to use it with confidence and ease in future lessons.

In this lesson, students devise their own system for grouping the shapes. They are encouraged to identify different properties of the various shapes and to practise their use of mathematical terminology.

To help students sort the shapes, they can trace the shapes onto paper, cut them out and move them between categories while they are developing their classification system. If you decide to run the lesson this way, students will require a pair of scissors each.

Lesson Outline

1. **Introducing the MATHOMAT—free play**

Ask students to use their MATHOMAT to make some designs of their choice and name each of the shapes used.

Include a brief sharing and discussion time to allow students to display their work and to alert other students to some of the possibilities.

2. **Students group shapes according to their own choice of categories**

This activity can be done individually or in groups.

Challenge students to find their own way of grouping the shapes and to produce a display of their results.

There are at least two ways to do this activity—which one you choose will depend on many factors including the year level of the students.

Students can trace all the MATHOMAT shapes onto a single sheet of paper, cut them out with scissors, decide on their categories as they try to sort the shapes, and finally record what they have done by drawing their groups onto a sheet of paper or a poster.

Alternatively, students can decide on their categories in advance, rule columns on a sheet of paper—using each category as a heading—and then draw each MATHOMAT shape directly under the appropriate heading.

In either case, all students should be prepared to describe their categories orally, while older students should also describe their categories in writing.

Do not insist that every shape is used, as some students may find the number of shapes overwhelming.

A few of the many possible ways of grouping the shapes are listed below:
- shapes with straight edges, shapes without straight edges;
- according to the number of vertices;
- shapes which contain parallel lines, shapes which do not; and
- shapes which contain at least two sides of equal length, shapes which do not.

Students often choose quite different and unexpected ways of grouping the shapes. This gives you a glimpse of what students see as compelling or pertinent properties of shapes and can suggest important features to discuss further with the class.

This activity provides an excellent opportunity for students to informally develop mathematical terminology.

3. Sharing and discussion

Select a few students to display their way of grouping the shapes.

Younger students can explain how they grouped their shapes to the rest of the class. With older students, the rest of the class can be challenged to come up with their own (oral or written) descriptions of the categories of the groupings shown.

Students will benefit from the opportunity to explain their sorting categories verbally. They will gain confidence in geometrical terminology and learn that other students may see different features as important when classifying the shapes.

4. (Optional extension) Guess My Family

This is a game for two or more players, which can also be played by the whole class.

A student chooses one of their (hidden) families of shapes and says 'I have chosen a family. I will answer yes or no if you ask me if a shape is a member of my family. I challenge you to name my family in as few questions as you can!'

The other students take it in turns to ask questions such as 'Is shape number 5 in your family?' or 'Do all the shapes in your family have straight edges?' The game ends when a student can correctly say 'Your family is …'. By playing this game, students will be forced to become more precise in their use of mathematical terminology, as well as become more aware of the properties of the shapes with which they are dealing.

5. (Further extension—if time available) creating attractive designs with the MATHOMAT

This is an extension of the first part of this lesson.

Challenge students to produce an attractive design using one or more MATHOMAT shapes. Ask students to list the numbers of the shapes used so that other students can reproduce their designs easily if they wish.

Encourage students to spend some time creating their designs. Their best designs can then be drawn on good quality paper, at home or in class. These designs can then be displayed and discussed in class at a later time.

Some examples of attractive designs can be found on page 7 of the MATHOMAT instruction book. A few of these are included below and overleaf.

Shape 12 only

Shapes 16, 18, 19

Shapes 16, 19, 38

Shapes 16, 18, 19, 24

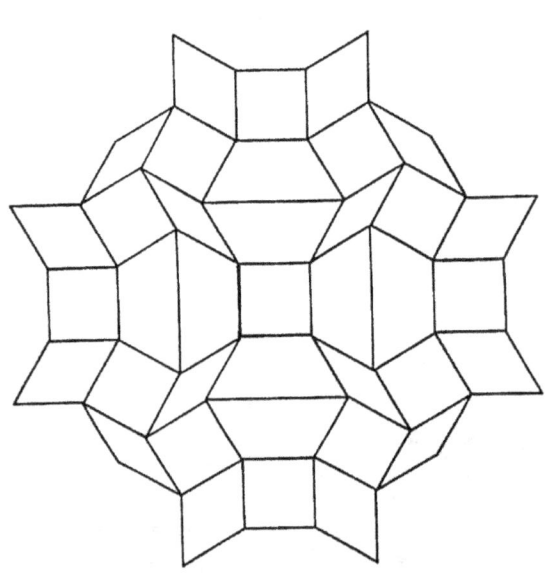

LESSON 2

Tiles, Tiles and More Tiles

Years 4 to 9

Patterns Using Transformations

This lesson fosters appreciation of the role of mathematics in art. It also provides students with the opportunity to demonstrate their creativity and gain personal satisfaction by drawing their own geometrical designs. Students can also develop their skills by transforming basic stencil shapes.

In this lesson students will:

- investigate the mathematics of decorative patterns;
- create decorative patterns using tessellations;
- identify and use transformations; and
- develop their knowledge of mathematical terminology.

Materials Required

For each student:

- a MATHOMAT;
- unlined paper (scrap paper will do);
- a sharp pencil;
- an eraser; and
- colouring materials such as felt-tip pens, pencils, crayons (optional).

Additional materials:
- examples of tessellations, including some by M. C. Escher.

Lesson Summary

- An introduction to tessellations, including examples of M. C. Escher's work;
- finding which MATHOMAT shapes tessellate using only one shape;
- producing tessellations using two or more shapes; and
- (optional extension) students produce their own Escher-style tessellations.

For the Teacher

A *tessellation* is a pattern which completely covers a surface or plane without any gaps or overlapping of the shapes used.

The challenge for students in this lesson is to systematically find which MATHOMAT shapes can be used—alone or in combination with other shapes—to tessellate the plane.

The lesson provides opportunities for students to discuss shapes (at an appropriate level) and to classify them according to their properties (such as whether or not they have all their sides of equal length, whether or not they possess parallel sides). With older students, some of the terminology of transformation geometry can also be introduced.

The extension activity, which can be completed at home, allows students to further express their creativity.

This lesson will need to be continued over a number of class periods if all aspects are to be covered.

In this lesson, encourage students to use a sharp pencil instead of a pen so that lines can be erased easily.

You will need to collect examples of tessellations (including some by M. C. Escher) to show the students. You may wish to produce one or more overhead transparencies of examples. Some examples which can be used are included in the Lesson Outline.

Lesson Outline

1. An introduction to tessellations—including viewing examples of M.C. Escher's work

Explain to students that a *tessellation* is a pattern which completely covers a surface or plane without any gaps or overlapping of the shapes used.

Some (boring!) tessellations include the types of tilings on most bathroom floors.

More exciting examples include the tilings produced by the Moors in places such as the Alhambra in Spain—an example of such a tiling is reproduced here.

The famous artist M. C Escher (1898–1972) derived much of his inspiration for space-filling designs from his first visit to the Alhambra in 1922. However, unlike the Moors, who were forbidden to use 'graven images' and who therefore only used geometric shapes for their tiling patterns, Escher attempted to completely cover the plane (i.e. create tessellations) with shapes which represented objects, such as animals or birds.

Most of Escher's work—which does not only consist of space filling designs—is mathematical. It is now widely available—for example as posters, in books, on coffee mugs, on the 'fifteen puzzle', on T-shirts, as jigsaw puzzles.

Two of Escher's space filling designs have been reproduced below, but you will probably want to collect your own examples to show your class.

 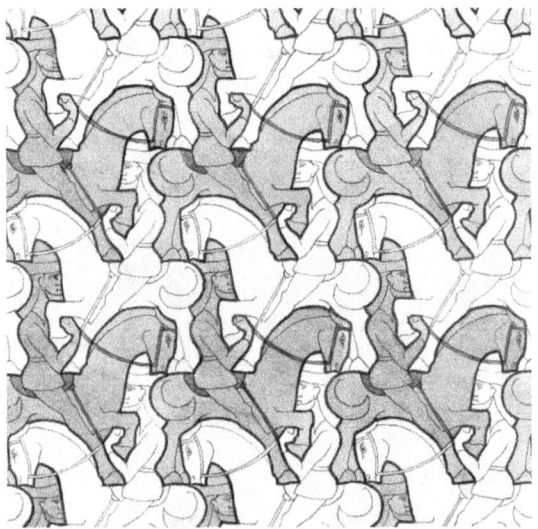

M. C. Escher's System ID   M. C. Escher's System IVB

© 1998 Cordon Art. V.V. - Baan - Holland All rights Reserved.

2. Finding which MATHOMAT shapes tessellate using one shape at a time

Ask students to find which of the MATHOMAT shapes tessellate, using just one shape at a time.

Students can work individually or in groups to classify the shapes into two categories—those which do tessellate by themselves and those which don't.

Working in groups allows this preliminary task to be completed more quickly and also encourages students to discuss their work with one another, thus helping them to develop terminology related to the shapes they are using.

3. Sharing and discussion

When most groups have completed the task, ask the class to share and discuss their solutions.

This discussion provides an excellent opportunity for students to revise terminology related to polygons—for example, the fact that a *regular* polygon is one which has all its sides of equal length and all its angles equal.

During the discussion, students will learn that there are only three *regular* polygons which can be used to completely cover the plane using just one shape at a time—the square, the equilateral triangle and the regular hexagon. These are reproduced below.

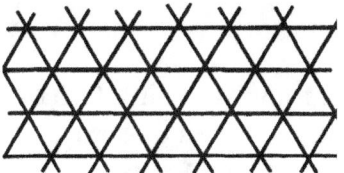  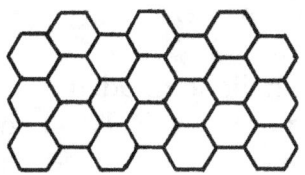

In addition, every convex quadrilateral and every triangle tessellates.

Some examples of the tiling patterns which can be formed using triangles and quadrilaterals on the MATHOMAT are reproduced below.

Isosceles Triangles   Rectangles

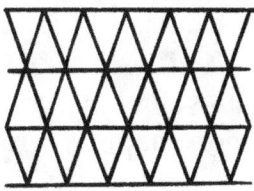 

Quadrilaterals   Right Angled Triangles

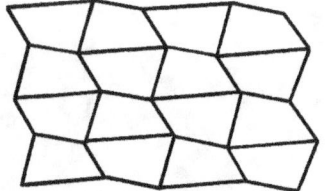 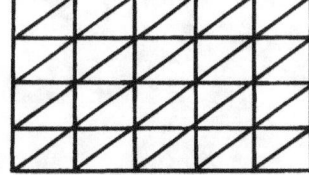

4. (Optional extension for older students) introducing transformation geometry

For older students, this can be an appropriate time to introduce some terminology related to transformation geometry. All of the above tessellations (including the two examples by M.C. Escher) can be produced by starting with just one shape and *transforming* it by means of a combination of *translations, reflections,* and *rotations*.

Choose a tessellation using just one shape—it is best to use interesting ones like the examples by M. C. Escher for this activity. Ask students to select two copies of the shape, one near the centre of the design and one near the edge. Challenge students to find how to transform the shape near the centre into the one near the edge, using a combination of translations, reflections and rotations.

Students who have no previous experience with translations, reflections and rotations would need to do some preliminary activities before tackling this task. They might be also interested to know that certain translations and reflections combine to give the last remaining possible transformation which preserves length—namely the *glide reflection*. Most students are unlikely to have much experience of glide reflections, whereas they are usually familiar with translations, reflections and rotations.

5. Producing tessellations using two or more shapes

Homogeneous tessellations are ones which use two or more regular polygons to tessellate the plane in such a way that the pattern formed at each vertex is the same.

Challenge students to produce as many tessellations as they can using two or more MATHOMAT shapes in such a way that the pattern formed at each vertex is the same—i.e. challenge them to find as many homogeneous tessellations as possible.

Altogether, there are eight homogeneous tessellations—they are reproduced opposite.

It is possible to produce the first six of these using MATHOMAT shapes 32 (equilateral triangle), 18 (square), 20 (regular hexagon) and 22 (regular octagon), which all have the same side length

In order to produce the last two of these homogeneous tessellations, you need to construct a regular dodecagon using the half dodecagon shape 39 which has the same side length as the other regular polygons.

Squares and Triangles

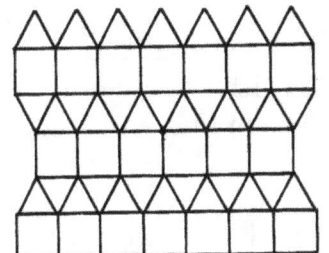 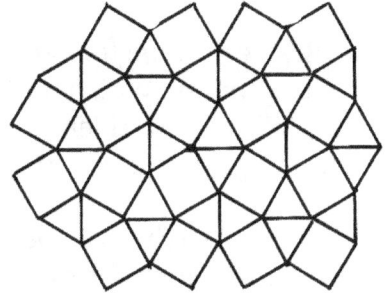

Hexagons and Triangles

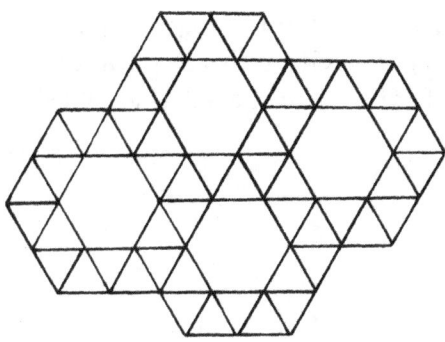 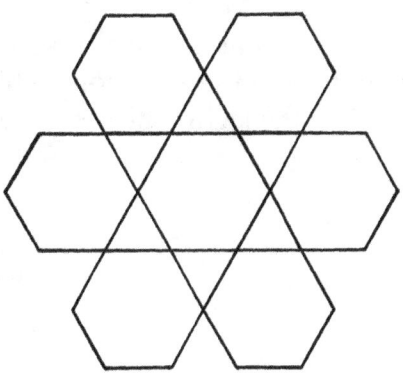

Octagons and Squares   Hexagons, Squares and Triangles

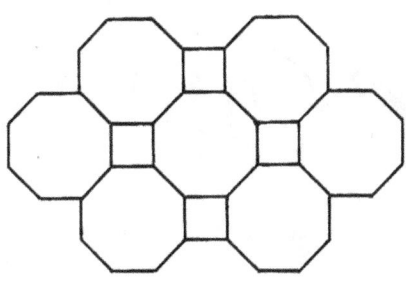 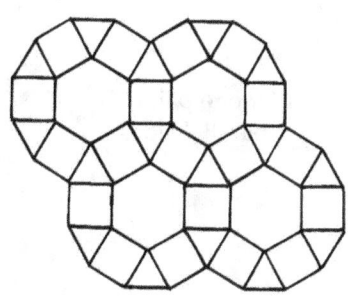

Dodecagons, Hexagons, Squares and Triangles   Dodecagons and Triangles

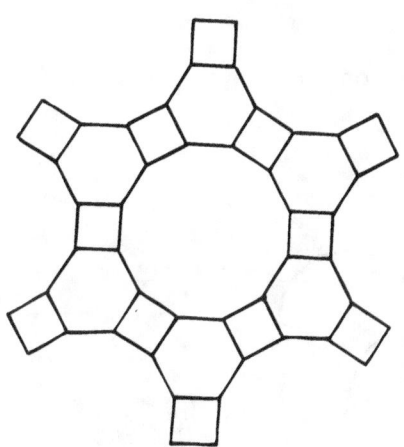 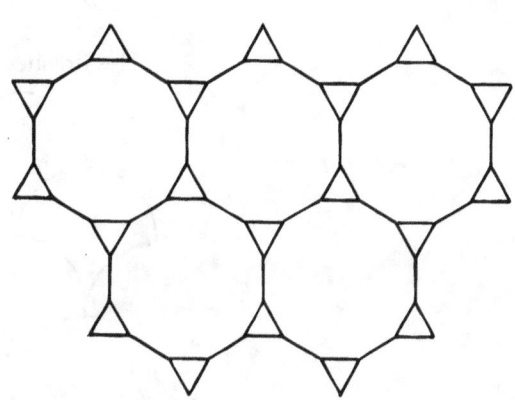

6. (Optional extension) students produce their own Escher-style tessellations.

The simplest technique for producing an Escher-style tessellation is to start with any tessellation which uses a single shape which has at least one pair of parallel sides of equal length—e.g. a square, a rhombus, a parallelogram, a regular hexagon, or a rectangle.

The technique is to change one side and then alter the parallel side in the same way, as shown in the example below. This procedure can be repeated for all pairs of parallel sides if desired.
Ask students to use this technique to design an Escher-type shape which tessellates. It takes some time and quite a bit of experimentation to produce an attractive shape which tessellates. Students may need to experiment with several different tessellations which use polygons with pairs of parallel sides and follow the technique described above before they find a satisfactory shape.

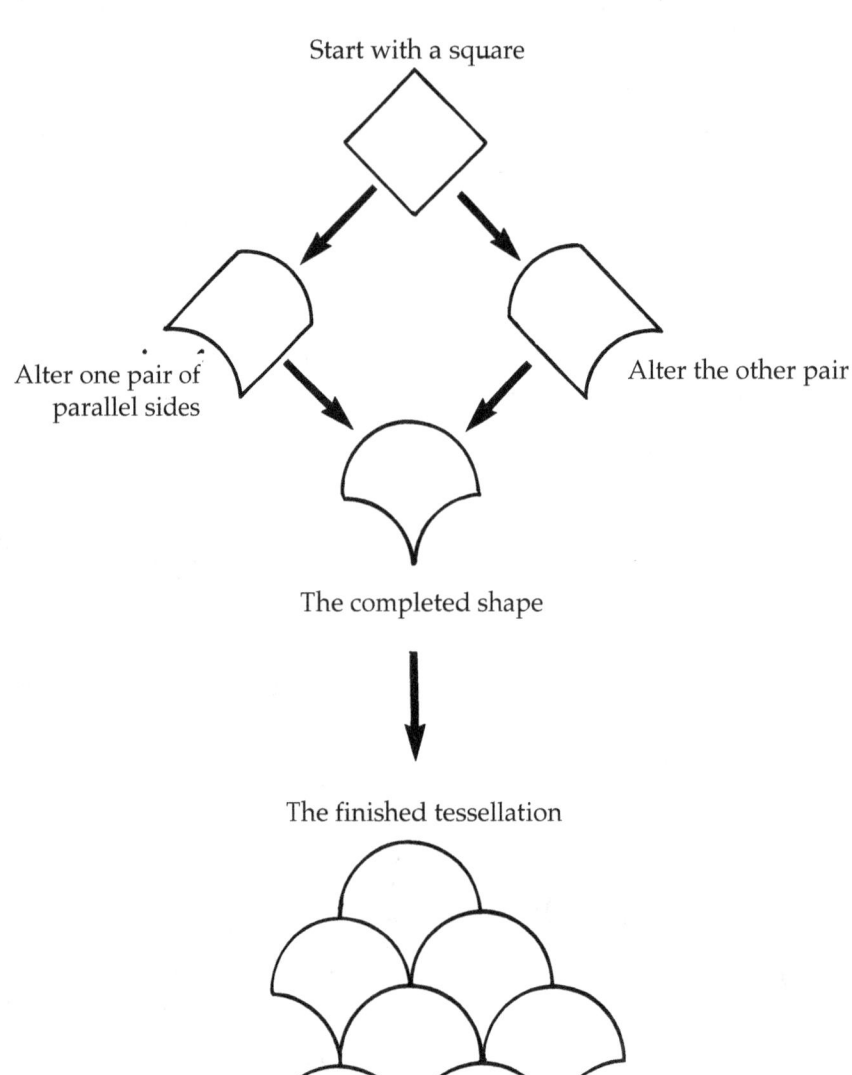

Once students have decided on their shape, the simplest way to produce a tessellation using their design is to follow the steps below.

Step 1: Trace one copy of the shape onto the original tessellation somewhere near the centre of the page, making sure it 'fits onto' the original shape. It is best to use a dark pen or a soft pencil so that the design will be clearly visible in Step 2 below.

Step 2: Place an unlined sheet of paper over the tessellation and trace the design onto the paper.

Step 3: Move the top sheet of paper until the traced design 'fits onto' one of the adjacent shapes on the original tessellation. Trace the shape again—this will give you a second (tessellating) copy of the design on the top sheet of paper.

Step 4: Repeat Step 3 until the tessellation is complete—you may need to 'move to a new place' on the sheet as parts of the tessellation are completed.

This method of producing the tessellation avoids the need to erase gridlines from the final copy.

Students may wish to colour their tessellation, taking care to produce a repeating pattern of colours. (While finding repeating patterns of colour for tessellations in general is itself a mathematical problem, older students can usually find a way to create a repeating pattern of colours for the particular case of their own tessellation.)

As it takes a long time to produce an attractive shape and even longer to produce the final design, students can be asked to complete this as a homework task.

7. Other possible extensions

There are many possible extensions of this lesson. A Deakin University postgraduate student, Sally Wilson, recently developed and taught a four lesson unit of work based on tessellations to a Year 4 class.

Students began by using the MATHOMAT to make symmetrical patterns and moved through a variety of activities, culminating with the production of a class quilt which was presented at the school assembly. As part of their activities, students manipulated polygons on a magnetic board to form tessellations, drafted a design for their quilt block, made a polygon template, chose suitable fabric and accurately cut out the polygons for the quilt block, and finally sewed fabric polygons together to form the class quilt. Materials used included the MATHOMAT, magnetic polygonal pattern blocks and a magnetic board, quilting and patchwork books and brickwork samples, example of tessellations produced by children of the same age (obtained from the internet—see references below), as well as a 'Big Book' produced by Sally for use with the class.

References

Escher, M. C. (1967). *The Graphic Work of M. C. Escher.* New York: Ballantine Books.

http://forum.swarthmore.edu/trscavo/tangrams/activities.html

http://mathcentral.uregina.ca/RR/database/RR.09.96/archamb1.html

http://www.quiltgallery.com/starred.html

http://ttsw.com/foundations/MiniQuilts/MiniGeese/html

http://www.jinneybeyer.com/blocks/block15pc.html

http://www.worldofescher.com/

Mottershead, L. (1977). *Metamorphosis: A Source Book of Mathematical Discovery.* Sydney: John Wiley.

Ranucci, E. R. & Teeters, J. L. (1977). *Creating Escher-Type Drawings.* Palo Alto, CA: Creative Publications.

Robinson, J. (1992). *Tessellations.* Durango, CO: Animas Quilts Publishing.

Schattschneider, D. (1990). *M. C. Escher: Visions of Symmetry.* New York: W. H. Freeman.

Seymour, D. (1989). *Tessellation Masters.* Palo Alto, CA: Dale Seymour Publications.

LESSON 3

Don't Be Square!

Years 5 to 9

Parallel Lines and Isometric Grids

This lesson presents some activities for student exploration of the MATHOMAT drawing guides. Students construct an isometric grid and use it to represent three-dimensional shapes.

In this lesson students will:

- construct parallel lines;
- construct isometric grids;
- represent three-dimensional shapes on paper; and
- (optional) attempt to solve a non-routine problem which involves constructing and recording shapes.

Materials Required

For each student:

- a MATHOMAT;
- unlined paper (scrap paper will do);
- blocks or plastic interlocking cubes—about 16 for each student;
- fine-point pens or pencils—at least two colours;
- crayons or felt-tip pens for colouring;
- a copy of Worksheet 3.1, Making Shapes; and
- (optional for older students) a copy of Handout 3.1, How to Draw an Isometric Grid.

For each group of four students:

- a set of eight three-dimensional models constructed from interlocking blocks—you will need to construct these prior to the lesson (see the diagram in part 3 of the Lesson Outline).

Additional materials:

- an overhead projector transparency of Drawing Three-Dimensional Shapes—see Transparency 3.1.

Lesson Summary

- Drawing parallel lines and parallelograms; constructing an isometric grid;
- drawing representations of three-dimensional shapes on an isometric grid;
- constructing three-dimensional models from two-dimensional drawings; and
- (optional) attempting the Four-Cube Houses problem.

For the Teacher

An isometric grid allows three-dimensional shapes to be represented in two dimensions.

The MATHOMAT template contains guides for drawing parallel lines and isometric grids—you will need to familiarise yourself with their operation before the lesson.

The guides for drawing isometric lines are on both sides of the MATHOMAT, but only those on the right side are labelled. Both sets of isometric guides are inclined at 30 degrees to the rulers on the sides of the MATHOMAT.

The labelled guides for drawing parallel lines are on the right hand side of the MATHOMAT and can be used to produce lines 1 cm (or multiples of 1 cm) apart.

You will need to give the students time to find and practise using the guides on the MATHOMAT before they attempt to draw grids on which to represent three-dimensional shapes.

A photocopy master of detailed instructions for constructing an isometric grid using the MATHOMAT is provided—see Handout 3.1, How to Draw an Isometric Grid. You will need to demonstrate this procedure to the class. For older students, you may wish to reproduce the sheet as a handout.

Lesson Outline

1. Drawing parallel lines

Start the lesson with a class discussion of the terms 'parallel' and 'parallelogram'. Demonstrate the use of the MATHOMAT parallel lines guide.

Ask students to use the guides to construct sets of parallel lines and parallelograms, and to make designs based on these.

Now ask students to construct a grid of horizontal and vertical lines 1 centimetre apart. (You might use the grids for Magic Squares or even allow the students to play Noughts and Crosses on them.)

Include a brief sharing and discussion time to allow students to display their work and to alert other students to some of the possibilities.

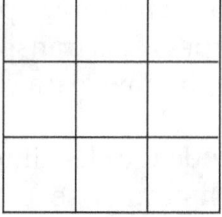

2. Constructing isometric grids

Discuss the features of an isometric grid with the class and compare it with the grid of horizontal and vertical lines drawn in the first part of this lesson. Use the step-by-step instructions in How to Draw an Isometric Grid (Handout 3.1) to carefully demonstrate to the class how the MATHOMAT *isometric lines* can be used to construct an isometric grid—some students will find this quite challenging. You may decide to distribute copies of Handout 3.1 to older students.

Ask students to construct their own isometric grid using this procedure.

If additional grids are required for the activities in later sections of this lesson, photocopies or commercially available isometric paper can be used.

3. Drawing three-dimensional shapes

An isometric grid can be used to represent a three-dimensional shape in two dimensions—the diagram shows a cube drawn on an isometric grid. The cube is viewed from above and three of its faces can be seen. Colouring and shading can be used to enhance isometrc drawings.

The representation of a cube on isometric grid paper

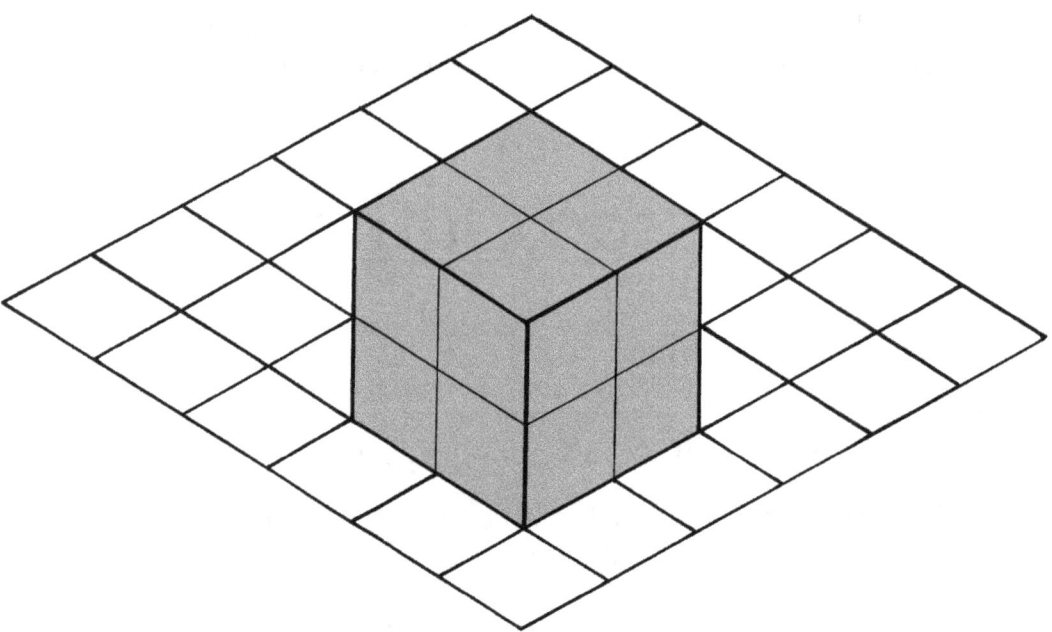

Discuss the representation of three-dimensional shapes in two dimensions— two examples are provided on Transparency 3.1, Drawing Three-Dimensional Shapes. This transparency also contains a blank isometric grid which you can use to draw extra shapes.

Divide the class into groups with about four students in each group. Give each group a set of the eight three-dimensional models that you have constructed from sets of interlocking cubes (see Materials Required— examples of the models are shown below).

Some shapes suitable for students to represent on isometric grids

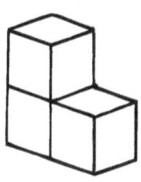 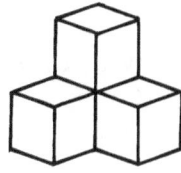 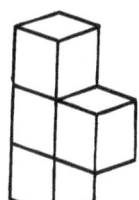 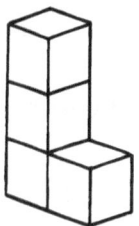

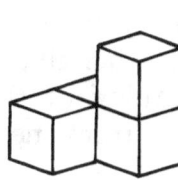 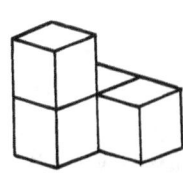 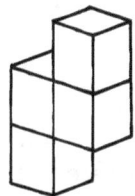 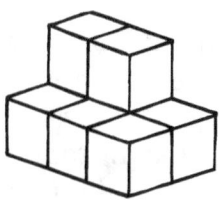

Allow students to handle the models, pull them apart and reconstruct them—they will gain familiarity with each shape, which will assist them with its representation.

Ask each group to share the task of representing the set of eight models on their pieces of isometric paper—it is not necessary for each student to represent each model.

Some students may wish to construct and represent their own shapes. As an optional extension, students may use isometric grids to draw challenging shapes for each other to construct.

After most groups have completed their drawings, select students to display their drawings to the rest of the class.

Compare the different ways in which each shape is represented—there are several valid ways in which each may be represented.

4. Constructing shapes from drawings

Distribute Worksheet 3.1, Making Shapes, and ask students to construct the shapes shown. This will require them to determine the number of cubes required to construct each shape—an interesting task when not all cubes are visible.

5. (Optional) Four-Cube Houses

The problem Four-Cube Houses challenges students to find and construct all shapes that can be formed, under certain conditions, from four identical interlocking cubes. In order to keep track of which cubes have been constructed, it is useful to record these on paper. In this lesson, students can be asked to represent each shape on isometric grid paper.

In the delightful article Four-Cube Houses, Freudenthal (1980) describes how this problem was introduced to a third grade class in the Netherlands using the well-known Dutch children's TV character Paulus the Forest Midget.

> There is restlessness in the midget town. Some houses are more beautiful than others. Paulus is called in as a troubleshooter. He proposes to rebuild the town. The midgets will live pairwise in houses, each consisting of a drawing room, a kitchen, and two bedrooms. All rooms are to be (congruent) cubes, and each house will be built from four cubes, which touch each other along complete faces …. It would be a dull town if all the houses were the same shape. (Freudenthal,1980, p. 12)

How many different houses can the midgets build?

In order to solve this problem, students will need to agree on some 'ground rules', such as the prohibition of cantilever houses (i.e. ones with 'overhanging" rooms) as well as agreeing on what constitutes 'different'—a good rule for this is that mirror images are different, but houses which can be obtained from one another through a rotation are not. Also, we are only interested in the arrangement of rooms, not whether it is a bedroom or bathroom.

Under these rules there are twelve different houses—students may need the best part of a lesson to find them all and establish a convincing argument why there are no more possible. It is well worth challenging students to find such a convincing argument and in the process find a good way of breaking the problem into sub-problems. This can lead to an excellent class discussion of the different ways in which groups classified their houses.

With older students, a good introduction to the problem is to set the context as a new ski village, which is being built using pre-fabricated houses transported from elsewhere.

Reference

Freudenthal, H. (1980). Four-cube houses. *For the Learning of Mathematics*, *1* (2), 12-13.

Drawing Three-Dimensional Shapes

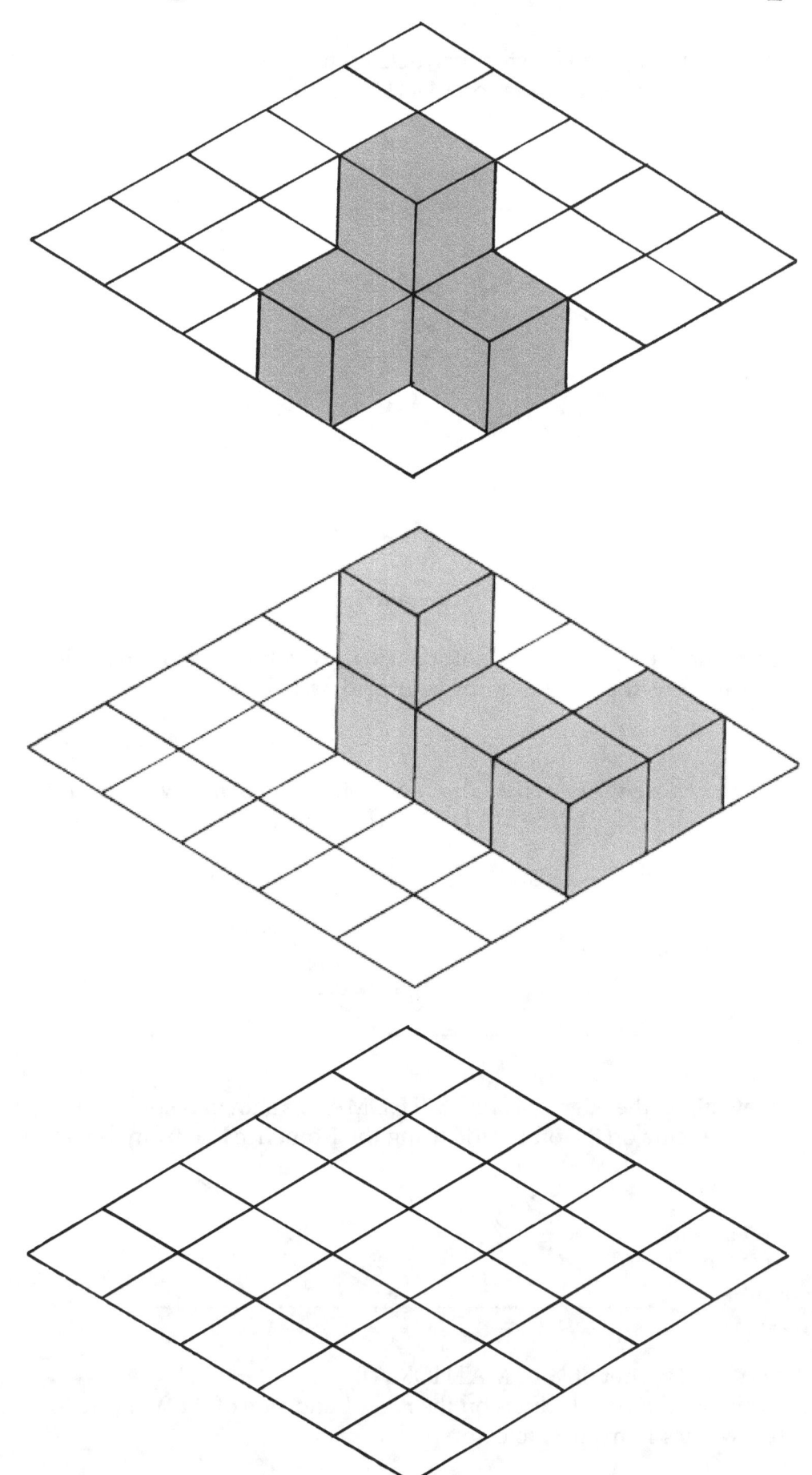

How to Draw an Isometric Grid

This sheet contains step-by-step instructions for drawing an isometric grid using the isometric line guides on MATHOMAT—a completed grid is shown in the following diagram.

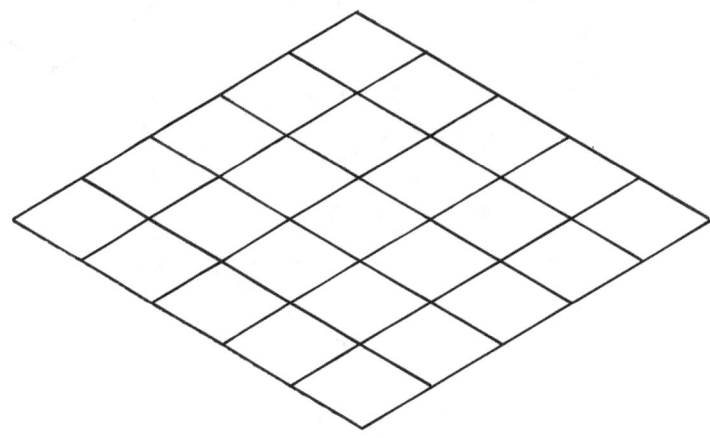

An isometric grid

1. Using unlined paper and a soft pencil, draw a horizontal line. This line, which forms the 'base line' for your grid, will later be erased.

2. Locate the *isometric line* near the top left corner of your MATHOMAT.

3. Superimpose the *isometric line* onto the horizontal line with the arrow head on the edge of the MATHOMAT oriented as shown in the next diagram.

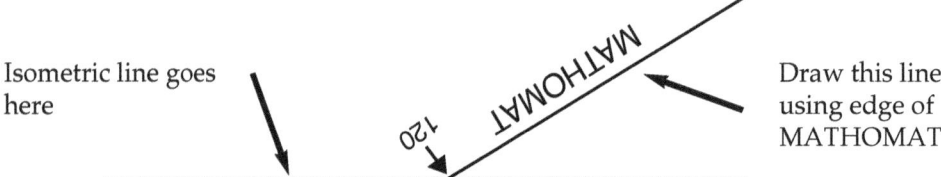

4. Draw along the edge of your MATHOMAT as shown below.
5. Do the same on the other side using the isometric line from the bottom

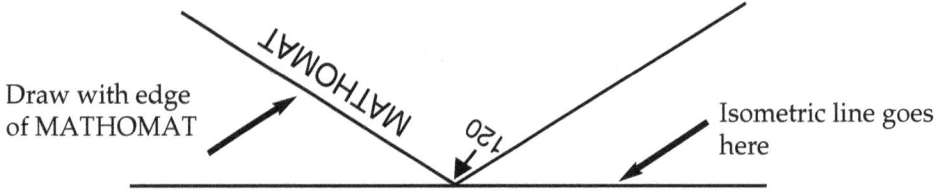

   left hand corner of your MATHOMAT.
6. Now use the parallel lines on the right-hand side of the MATHOMAT to draw lines 1 cm apart to complete the grid.

Making Shapes

Each diagram shows a solid three-dimensional shape on an isometric grid—only external edges of the shapes are shown. Beside each diagram write the

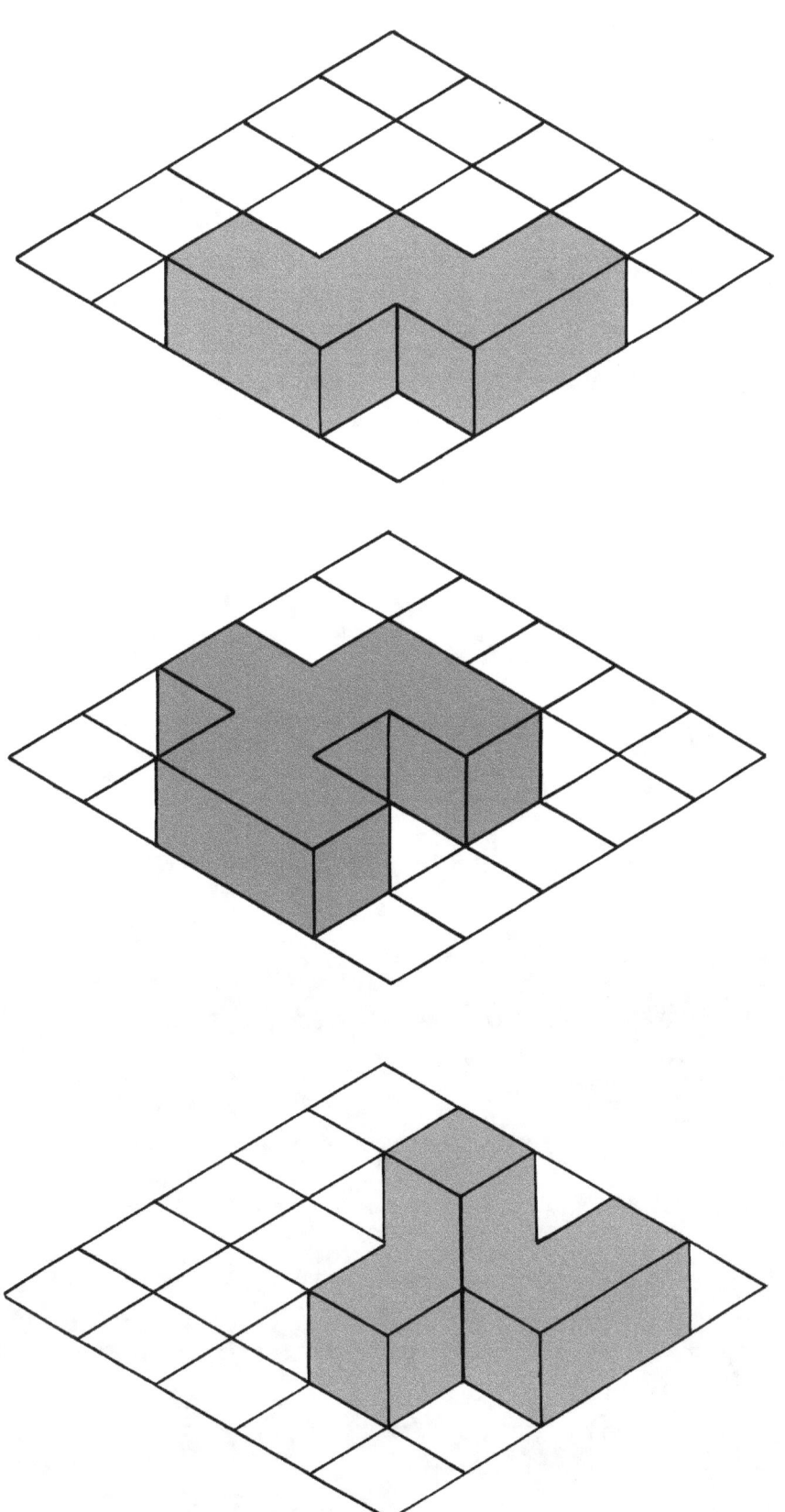

LESSON 4

Bigger and Bigger

Years 5 to 9

Enlarging Figures to Construct Polyhedra Nets

This lesson involves students using their MATHOMAT to enlarge regular polygons to produce nets of selected polyhedra, which are then used to construct three-dimensional models. The activities allow students to develop techniques for accurate construction.

In this lesson students will:

- enlarge two-dimensional figures;

- develop techniques for accurate construction;

- develop their knowledge of mathematical terminology;

- make three-dimensional models from nets; and

- (for older students) visualise, describe and compare the numbers of faces, edges and vertices of polyhedra.

Materials Required

For each student:

- a MATHOMAT;
- a fine-point pen and a sharp pencil;
- lightweight card, approximately A4 size;
- scissors;
- sticky tape;
- a copy of Handout 4.1, The Five Platonic Solids—alternatively this can be reproduced on an overhead projector transparency for display to the entire class; and
- (optional) a copy of Handout 4.2, How to Enlarge Regular Polygons—see the next page for details.

Additional materials:

- (optional) commercial or 'home-made' examples of regular polyhedra—e.g. straw models, mobiles, models constructed from three-dimensional construction toys such as Polydron or Geoshapes.

Lesson Summary

- Using the MATHOMAT to enlarge regular polygons;
- an introduction to polyhedra;
- using the MATHOMAT to create nets and construct polyhedra; and
- (optional) investigating properties of polyhedra.

For the Teacher

This lesson involves students using their MATHOMAT to enlarge regular polygons. Instructions for enlarging regular polygons are given in Handout 4.2, How to Enlarge Regular Polygons. The technique differs slightly for polygons with odd and even numbers of sides.

You may wish to use the How to Enlarge Regular Polygons sheet as a handout, but you would still need to demonstrate the procedure to students.

Younger students can be shown how to enlarge an equilateral triangle and a square. Older students can be shown how to enlarge an equilateral triangle only and can then be challenged to generalise the method to other regular polygons.

Developing the process for enlarging the figures can motivate a discussion of many properties of plane figures, using appropriate terminology. For example, terms such as mid-point, vertex, parallel, intersection of lines, similar, congruent and scaling factor would arise naturally at the appropriate year level, while properties of regular polygons can also be explored.

Students use their enlargements to draw nets of selected regular polyhedra onto lightweight card, which can then be used to construct three-dimensional models. You need to decide which polyhedra students will construct.

Depending on the year level, you can introduce or revise a suitable selection of the terminology relating to polyhedra listed below.

- A *polyhedron* is a three-dimensional figure bounded by polygonal regions—i.e. it has polygons as its faces.

- A *regular polyhedron* has identical regular polygons for all its faces.

- A polyhedron is *convex* if, whenever you join up two points on the surface of the solid with a straight line, every point on the line is inside or on the surface of the solid.

There are only five possible regular convex polyhedra—this was discovered by the ancient Greeks. These five polyhedra are known as the *Platonic solids*. These solids and their nets are illustrated on Handout 4.1, The Five Platonic Solids, which also indicates suitable lengths for the edges in order to produce a fairly rigid solid whose net fits onto an A4 sized card.

You can either give each student a copy of Handout 4.1, or reproduce it on an overhead projector transparency for display to the entire class.

For younger students, this activity can be motivated by using the solids constructed to make mobiles and other decorations.

For older students, this lesson can also provide opportunities to investigate and discuss properties of polyhedra, such as the number of vertices, edges and faces and their relationship. Year 9 students can verify that Euler's formula applies to these solids.

The lesson provides an opportunity for students to develop techniques for accurate construction. The challenge for students is to produce accurate nets and to construct their solids as neatly as possible.

It is important that the enlarged shape used as the template for the net is constructed accurately. Make sure that students use a sharp pencil and are careful with their construction and cutting.

Students should always use a fine-point pen and the edge of the MATHOMAT to lightly score all fold lines. This is a very important step in constructing neat solids with sharp edges. However, it takes practice to achieve score lines which are sufficiently firm but which do not rip the card. Students should practise this on scrap pieces of card before scoring their nets. The fact that the resulting edges are marked in pen does not detract from the finished solid.

This lesson will need to be continued over a number of class periods if all aspects are to be covered.

Lesson Outline

1. Enlarging regular polygons

A technique for enlarging regular polygons is described in Handout 4.2, How to Enlarge Regular Polygons.

Younger students can be shown how to enlarge an equilateral triangle and a square.

Older students can be shown how to enlarge an equilateral triangle only and then be challenged to generalise the method to other regular polygons.

Begin the lesson by demonstrating the chosen technique(s) to the class.

The technique depends on the fact that for regular polygons with an odd number of sides the lines joining the vertices to the mid-points of the opposite sides intersect in a point, while for those with an even number of sides the diagonals joining opposite pairs of vertices intersect in a point.

Use the activity to motivate a class discussion on various properties of triangles. For example, older students should notice that the lines joining the vertices to the mid-points of opposite sides intersect in a point (as expected).

The sides of the enlarged triangle are parallel to those of the original triangle. (In fact this feature can be used to produce the new triangle, using the parallel line guides on the MATHOMAT. This can be done by drawing parallel lines at equal distances from the three sides of the original triangle and using the intersections of these lines as the vertices of the new triangle.)

There are many examples of similar triangles and isosceles triangles contained in the construction of the enlarged triangle—with older students these can be used to construct an argument to justify the fact that the new triangle is also equilateral.

Challenge students to enlarge various regular polygons from their MATHOMAT. After students have had some practice, ask them to produce enlargements with specified side lengths (this is difficult to do accurately and reasonable approximations should be accepted).

2. An introduction to polyhedra

The enlargement procedures developed in part 1 of this lesson will be used by students to draw nets and construct three-dimensional models.

The degree of detail and the number of models constructed will depend on the year level and the time available to pursue these aspects.

Begin with a discussion of the models you have selected for the students to construct. Depending on the year level, students can be introduced to some of the terminology for regular polyhedra—see page 33 for some definitions.

Show students some examples of commercial or 'home-made' regular polyhedra (e.g. straw models, mobiles, models constructed form the three-dimensional construction toys such as Polydron or Geoshapes, models from card made in other classes, or even any box in the shape of a cube).

Explain to students that the Greeks had already discovered that there are only five possible regular convex polyhedra—these are illustrated below and on Handout 4.1. Their names, apart from the cube, are derived from the Greek words for the number of faces—e.g. 'tetra' for 'four' and 'hedron' for 'face'.

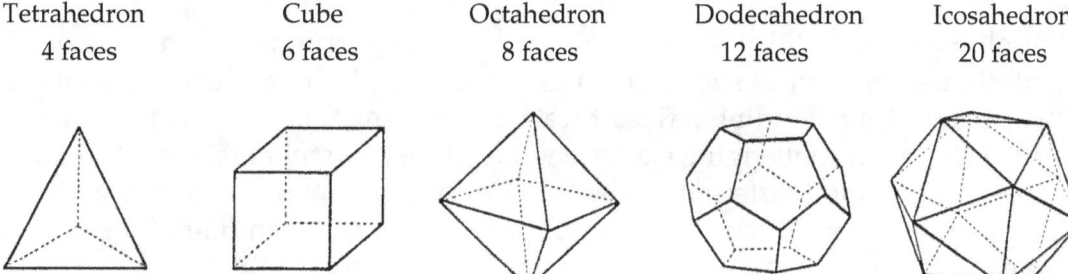

| Tetrahedron | Cube | Octahedron | Dodecahedron | Icosahedron |
| 4 faces | 6 faces | 8 faces | 12 faces | 20 faces |

These five polyhedra are known as the *Platonic solids* and have been the subject of interest to mankind for a very long time. For example, Kepler at first believed that, as part of God's plan, the motion of the planets was related to the Platonic solids.

3. Using the MATHOMAT to create nets and construct polyhedra

The five Platonic solids all have faces which are either equilateral triangles, squares or regular pentagons.

Nets for each of the Platonic solids, together with approximate side lengths to allow comfortable construction from an A4 sheet of card, are shown on Handout 4.1, The Five Platonic Solids.

Depending on the year level and the time available, select one or more of the polyhedra for students to construct (or allow students to select their own). The first step in the construction of the nets is to use the MATHOMAT to draw and then enlarge the appropriate shape to a suitable size for constructing the solid. The enlarged shape should be drawn on a piece of card, which can then be cut out and used as a template to construct the net.

Before cutting out the net, students should lightly score their nets by using a fine-point pen and the edge of the MATHOMAT to lightly rule over each fold line on their net. This will result in neat, sharp edges on their solid.

After carefully cutting out their nets, students can use sticky tape to secure the faces.

For a better result (but one which takes a great deal more time and effort!) students can construct flaps on appropriate faces and use glue instead of sticky tape for the construction.

4. (Optional) investigating properties of polyhedra

A brief discussion of the polyhedra can include counting the faces and checking that—apart from the cube—their names represent the number of faces. Other terminology such as parallel edges, parallel faces, vertices, may also arise in the discussion. For younger students, this activity can be motivated by using the models constructed to make mobiles or other decorations.

For older students, this lesson can also provide opportunities to investigate and discuss properties such as the number of vertices, edges and faces and their relationship. Finding efficient ways of counting the numbers of edges and vertices is a challenging exercise which develops students' visualisation skills. Encouraging different students to explain their ways of counting can lead to an excellent discussion and a much better understanding of the solids.

Year 9 students can verify that Euler's formula applies to these solids.

[Euler's formula for simply connected solids states that

$$F + V - E = 2$$

where F is the number of faces, V the number of vertices and E the number of

The Five Platonic Solids

The five regular convex polyhedra (also known as the Platonic Solids) and their nets are drawn below. Next to each net is a suggested side length for each shape which produces a fairly rigid solid whose net fits onto an A4 sized card.

The Tetrahedron

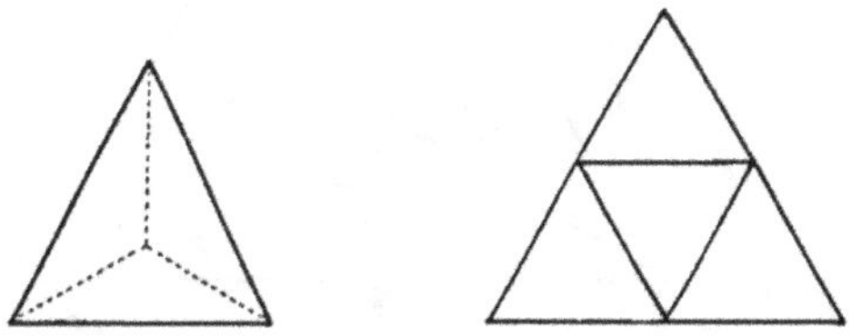

9 cm

The Cube

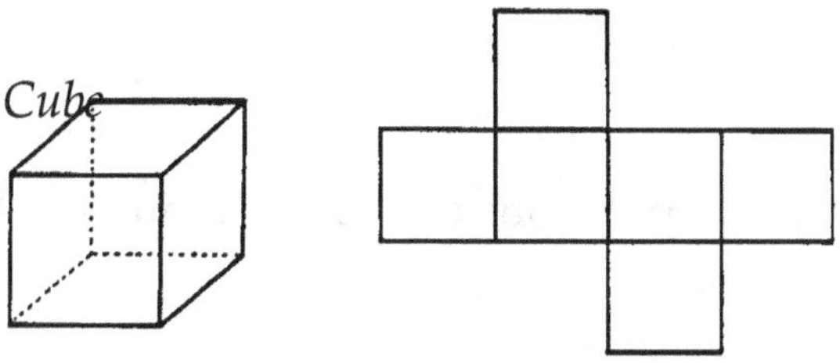

6 cm

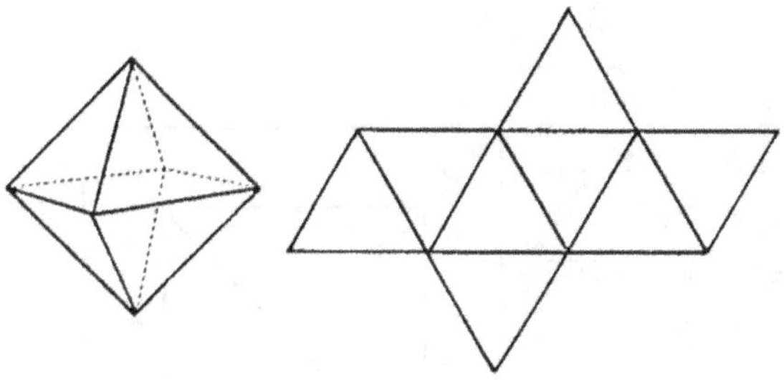

The Octahedron

6 cm

The Dodecahedron

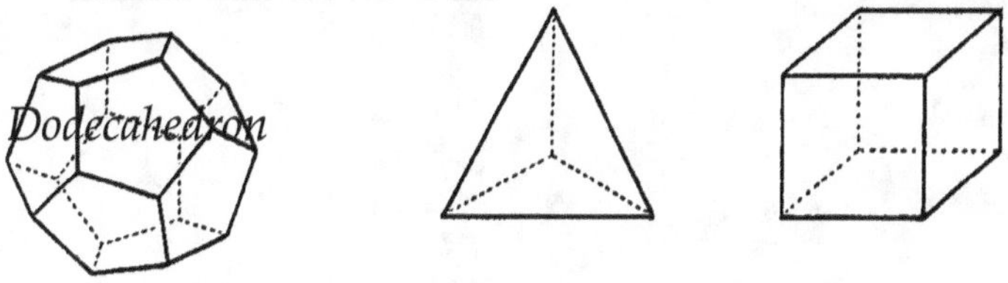

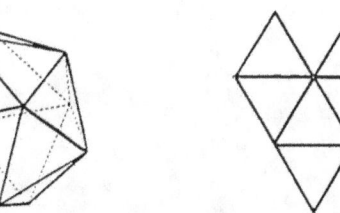

3.5cm

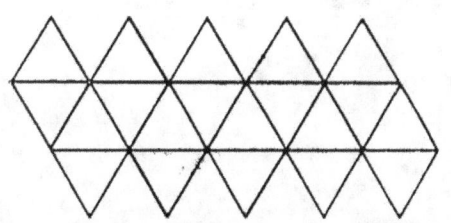

(or 4.5 cm with

two halves of the

net on a sheet of

How to Enlarge Regular Polygons

How to enlarge an equilateral triangle

Use your MATHOMAT to draw an equilateral triangle (shape 23) and mark the mid-points of the sides.

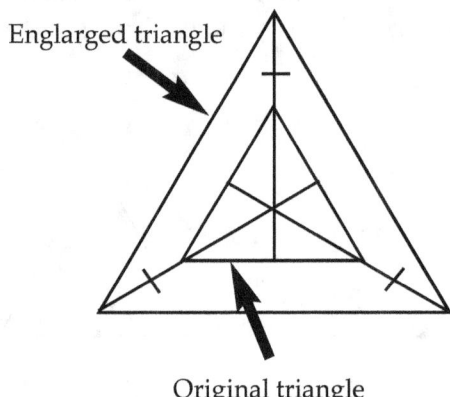

Englarged triangle

Original triangle

Join the mid-points of the sides to the vertices and continue your line beyond each vertex.

Mark off equal lengths beyond the vertex on each of these lines.

Join these points to make your new enlarged equilateral triangle.

This procedure can be used for all regular polygons with an odd number of sides.

How to enlarge a square

To enlarge a square, use shape 1 and repeat the same procedure as for the triangle, but join pairs of opposite vertices instead of mid-points and vertices—see diagram.

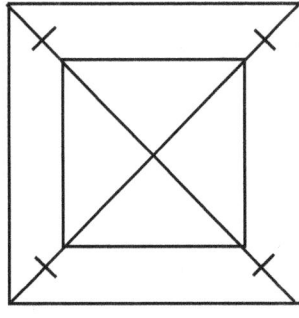

This procedure can be used for all regular polygons with an even number of sides.

LESSON 5

This Looks Like That!

Years 4 to 8

Investigating Symmetry

This lesson involves students in investigating the symmetry of MATHOMAT and other shapes and using MATHOMAT shapes to create two-dimensional symmetrical shapes and patterns.

In this lesson students will:

- investigate lines of symmetry in two-dimensional shapes; and

- classify shapes according to the number of lines of symmetry.

Materials Required

For each student:

- a MATHOMAT;

- unlined paper (scrap paper will do);

- a copy of the Worksheet 5.1, Lines of Symmetry in Complex Shapes (a photocopy master is provided at the end of this lesson); and

- fine-point pens or pencils.

Additional materials:

- one overhead projector version or photocopies for each group of students of Transparency 5.1, Lines of Symmetry (a photocopy master is provided at the end of this lesson).

Lesson Summary

- Identifying lines of symmetry on MATHOMAT shapes;

- classifying shapes according to the number of lines of symmetry they have;

- completing and constructing symmetrical two-dimensional shapes and patterns; and

- identifying lines of symmetry in more complex shapes.

For the Teacher

A line (or axis) of symmetry in a figure is a line that divides the figure into two identical parts, which are mirror images of one another. Any point of the figure will have a corresponding (or image) point at an equal distance on the opposite side of the line of symmetry.

Some examples of figures which have one or more lines of symmetry are included in the Transparency 5.1, Lines of Symmetry at the end of this lesson. These can be either reproduced on an overhead projector transparency for class discussion or photo-copied for groups of students to look at and discuss.

This lesson provides opportunities for students to explore the lines of symmetry in the two-dimensional shapes on the MATHOMAT template and classify the shapes according to the number of lines of symmetry. For some shapes, the markings provided on their perimeter can be used to construct lines of symmetry. If desired, the sin/cos curve (number 31), the parabola (number 34) and the half dodecagon (number 39) can also be included here.

The 40 MATHOMAT shapes and curves include those which have no lines of symmetry (the scalene triangles), those which have one line of symmetry (the non-equilateral isosceles triangles, the trapezium, the sin/cos curve, the parabola and the half dodecagon), those which have two lines of symmetry (the ellipses, the rhombus and the non-square rectangles), those which have three, four, five, six or eight lines of symmetry (the regular polygons with the corresponding number of sides) and the circles which have infinitely many lines of symmetry. Depending on the year level, students should be encouraged to attempt to describe their results from the classification activity in general terms like that given above. This can form the basis of a valuable class discussion.

Following the classification activity, students can use their MATHOMAT to construct and create attractive symmetrical shapes and patterns, as well as identify lines of symmetry in more complex patterns.

Lesson Outline

1. Introducing lines of symmetry

Use an overhead projector transparency or photocopy of Transparency 5.1, Lines of Symmetry to introduce a class discussion about symmetry. This can also include: a discussion of everyday objects which have lines of symmetry (e.g. flowers, T-shirts when ironed flat, forks and spoons but not knives— this is stretching two-dimensions a bit); a brief investigation of the lines of symmetry of upper case letters of the alphabet; and a discussion of the fact one side of a person's face and its mirror image look decidedly odd!)

Students should be aware that some shapes might have no lines of symmetry while others might have infinitely many.

2. Identifying lines of symmetry in MATHOMAT shapes

Ask students to work individually or in groups to construct lines of symmetry for each of the MATHOMAT shapes.

Students can trace MATHOMAT shapes onto paper and draw lines of symmetry onto the shapes in order to find and record how many lines of symmetry each shape has. For some shapes, the markings provided on the perimeter of the shapes on the MATHOMAT can be used to construct lines of symmetry.

3. Classifying MATHOMAT shapes according to the number of lines of symmetry

Ask students to work in groups to classify the MATHOMAT shapes according to the number of lines of symmetry.

Each group should be encouraged to record and display their results in preparation for a class discussion. Students may wish to complete a table like the one shown on the following page.

There are many different ways to produce such a table and students should be encouraged to plan how to display their results. Tracing or gluing copies of the shapes onto the table (as in the table shown)—rather than just recording the shape numbers—has the advantage that it will encourage students to recognise general properties of the shapes. However, the table required to do this will be quite large. Younger students can produce an attractive poster at this stage. Older students can classify the shapes directly from the previous part of the activity and replace the drawings in the table by their descriptions in words of the types of shapes which would be found in each cell of the table.

As soon as most groups have completed their recordings or displays, hold a class discussion to compare results and attempt to come to an agreement on the types of shapes which have different numbers of lines of symmetry. This discussion can be valuable at all year levels in developing students' ability to use conventional geometric language to describe classes of shapes.

Sample table classifying MATHOMAT shapes according to numbers of lines of symmetry

Number of lines of symmetry	Shapes
0	36
1	33, 24
2	6
3	
4	
5	10
6	
7	
8	
∞	35

4. Identifying lines of symmetry in more complex shapes

Ask students to work individually or in groups to complete the Worksheet 5.1, Lines of Symmetry in Complex Shapes.

The first part asks students to complete diagrams showing half of a pattern which has been produced using MATHOMAT shapes and find the number of lines of symmetry for each complete pattern. The second part shows some diagrams which have been produced using a MATHOMAT and others which are photos of objects occurring in real life. Students are again asked to find the number of lines of symmetry for each diagram—of course the real life objects won't be perfect!

5. Creating symmetrical patterns

Ask students to create their own symmetrical patterns using their MATHOMAT. Older students can be asked to produce patterns with specified numbers of lines of symmetry.

References

Williams, G. (1971). *African Designs from Traditional Sources.* Dover Pictorial Archive Series. New York: Dover Publications.

Lines of Symmetry

Senufo wooden mask, Ivory Coast/Mali/Upper Volta
(Williams, 1971, p. 123). Reproduced with permission.

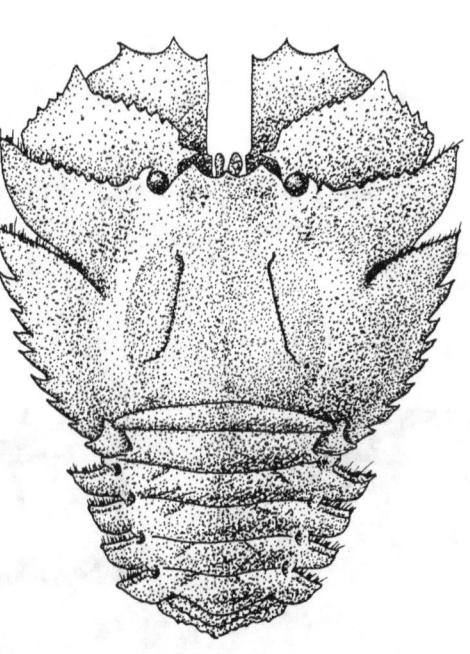

WORKSHEET 5.1

Lines of Symmetry in Complex Shapes

1. Each of the diagrams below is half of a pattern which has been produced using a MATHOMAT.

    a) Use your MATHOMAT to complete each of the diagrams below.

    b) For each of the completed patterns, find the number of lines of symmetry and record your answer in the space provided.

  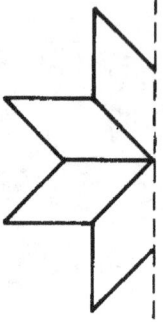

☐   ☐   ☐

2. For each of the diagrams below, find the number of lines of

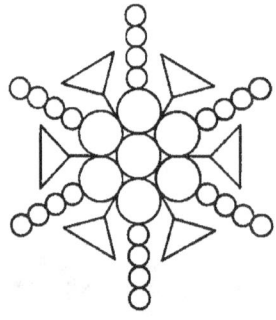

symmetry and record your answer in the space provided.

a) MATHOMAT DESIGN

☐   ☐   ☐

MATHS WITH MATHOMAT

LESSON 6

The Area is Right!

Years 4 to 8

Estimating and Measuring Areas

In this lesson students compare the areas of the individual MATHOMAT shapes, firstly by estimation and then by measurement. Students initially work with informal units and older students convert their answers into formal units.

MATHOMAT shapes are used to investigate packing problems—fitting objects such as soft-drink cans into containers.

In this lesson students will:

- use estimation to rank MATHOMAT shapes according to area;

- measure the area of the shapes by drawing them on grid paper and counting squares; and

- (optional extension) investigate the packing of

Materials Required

For each student:

- a MATHOMAT;

- unlined paper (scrap paper will do);

- fine-point pens or pencils; and

- grid paper of various sizes (photocopy masters for 5 mm and 2 mm grid paper are provided at the end of this lesson —see Handouts 6.2 and 6.3).

For each group of four students:

- a copy of The Area is Right! Entry Form (photocopy master provided—see Worksheet 6.1); and

- a copy of the Area of MATHOMAT Shapes sheet (a photo copy master is provided as Handout 6.1, although making a copy of this sheet for each group is optional—see later sections for details).

Lesson Summary

- Ranking MATHOMAT shapes by estimating their areas;

- measuring areas by tracing shapes on grid paper and counting squares; and

- (optional extension) investigating the packing of selected shapes into larger shapes.

For the Teacher

In this lesson students compare the areas of the individual MATHOMAT shapes.

This is done firstly by estimation and then by measurement.

In order to measure the areas in informal units, each shape is drawn on grid paper of appropriate size and the number of squares it covers is counted. Older students can convert their answers into formal units (cm^2 or mm^2).

Photocopy masters for both 5 mm and 2 mm grid paper are provided (see Handouts 6.2 and 6.3). It is only feasible to use 2 mm grids if the task of measuring is shared amongst a group of students and the students are able to take short cuts by calculating the area of rectangular portions within shapes. Depending on the year level of the students, you might use both the 5 mm and the 2 mm grids, or only use one of these, or only use the 2 mm grid when it is impossible to decide between the area of two shapes using the 5 mm grid.

A competitive game The Area is Right!, loosely based on a television quiz-show with a similar title, is used to add interest to the lesson.

To play the game, divide the class into groups with about four students in each group. Ask each group to use estimation to select and rank in order the ten MATHOMAT shapes with largest area. They trace and label these shapes in order on The Area is Right! Entry Form (Worksheet 6.1) and enter the shape number in the second column of the table provided. They should then also 'submit' their entries in a form suitable for display—e.g. write their rank ordering on the chalkboard. After a brief class discussion of similarities and differences between the 'entries', each group measures the areas of their selected shapes using grid paper and the class scores the entries to find the winning group.

The Area of MATHOMAT Shapes sheet (Handout 6.1) is a table of the actual areas of the MATHOMAT shapes which can assist you when the class is scoring the entries. (The ten largest MATHOMAT shapes, in descending order of area, are shapes 29, 3, 15, 4, 1, 9, 33, 21, 36, 10).

You may wish to organise the scoring of entries in a different way from that given in the Lesson Outline, in which case you may wish to give each group a copy of the Area of MATHOMAT Shapes sheet. Note that areas given in the 'Area in 5 mm squares' and 'Area in 2 mm squares' columns are approximations and the class will need to come to an agreement as to the degree of accuracy expected in order for area measurements to be regarded as 'correct'.

As an extension activity, the MATHOMAT shapes are used to investigate a realistic problem involving fitting soft-drink cans into containers.

Lesson Outline

1. Using estimation to rank MATHOMAT shapes according to area

Start the lesson with a brief class discussion on area.

Ask students to select the MATHOMAT shape which they think has the largest area and discuss reasons for their choices. Repeat this for the shape with the smallest area.

Explain to the students that their estimates of relative areas will be the basis for the game The Area is Right! Explain how to play the game, including the way in which the entry form is to be used.

Organise students into small groups with about four students in each group and give each group an entry form (Worksheet 6.1).

Ask each group to select and rank in order the ten MATHOMAT shapes with largest area, using estimation only—at this stage, counting squares is not allowed. As each group agrees on the selected shapes and their order ask them to trace and label these shapes, in order, on The Area is Right! Entry Form and enter the shape number in the second column of the table provided.

Each group must then also 'submit' their entries in a form suitable for display—e.g. by writing their rank ordering on the chalkboard.

As each group submits their entries, give them copies of the appropriate grid paper and ask them to start on part 2 of the lesson, measuring areas.

When all groups have submitted their entries, conduct a brief class discussion, comparing and contrasting the 'entries'.

2. Measuring areas

Ask each group to share the task of measuring the areas of their ten shapes among the members of the group—there is no need for each student to measure the area of each shape.

The areas of the MATHOMAT shapes can be measured by carefully drawing them onto a grid and counting squares (photocopy masters of 5 mm and 2 mm square grids are provided—see Handouts 6.2 and 6.3). For example, the area of the ellipse (shape 4) is 25 squares on the 5 mm grid paper as shown in the next diagram. Of course this is an approximation obtained by 'balancing out' incomplete squares which are shaded with those which are not.

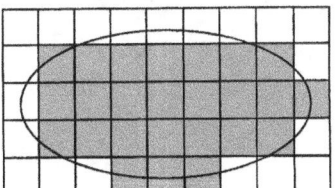

Measuring the area of shape 4

Ask students to record their results in the appropriate columns of the table on their group's The Area is Right! Entry Form.

Depending of the year level and the time available, the last two columns can be used for students to convert the areas to square centimetres or square millimetres.

4. Scoring the entries

Use a class discussion, based on the students' results from measuring the areas, to decide the ten MATHOMAT shapes with largest area and their correct ranked order. As some of these shapes are similar in area this will generate lively discussion and the class will need to come to an agreement as to the degree of accuracy expected in order for area measurements to be regarded as 'correct'.

Give each group a score based on the number of shapes they have in 'correct' rank order 'from the top'— e.g. if a group has the first six shapes in correct order, but their seventh shape is incorrect, they get a score of 6. The group with the highest score is declared the winner.

5. Optional modifications

The game may be modified in a number of ways. For example, the students may select and rank the ten smallest MATHOMAT shapes. Alternatively, the selection of sets of shapes for ranking could be based on geometric properties of shapes, such as:

- polygons;
- triangles;
- shapes with at least two side parallel; or
- ellipses and circles.

6. (Optional extension) a packing problem

Organise the students into groups and present them with the following problem.

Packing soft drink cans

Your task is to design an unusual and attractive container for soft drink cans. However, it is also important to consider how efficiently the cans are packed into the container.

You are trying to decide between a number of different shapes to use as the base of the container. These are represented on the MATHOMAT by shapes 8, 20, 24 and 23. On the same scale, the soft-drink cans are represented by MATHOMAT shape 14.

Investigate fitting shape 14 into the other shapes and decide which shape you would choose for the container, giving reasons.

For example, the cans might be packed into the triangle as shown below.

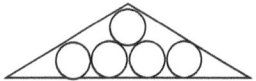

Extension for older students: Estimate the percentage of waste space for different shapes, using your earlier area measurements.

After the groups have tackled the problem, conduct a class discussion. Ask the groups to share the results of their investigations and give reasons for their choice of shape for the container.

As an appropriate follow-up of this problem, you may wish to discuss broader issues associated with packaging, particularly as exemplified by the packaging of articles that may be purchased in super-markets.

The Area is Right! Entry Form

GROUP   SCORE

In the space below, trace and lable the ten MATHOMAT shapes you estimate have the largest area. Start with the largest shape and then enter the others in order—as you do this, record each shape's number in the second column of the table.

Ranking by area	Shape Number	Area in 5 mm squares	Area in 2 mm squares	Area in cm^2	Area in mm^2
1					
2					
3					
4					
5					
6					
7					
8					
9					
10					

WORKSHEET 6.1

MATHS WITH MATHOMAT

53

Area of MATHOMAT Shapes

Shape number	Area in 2 mm squares	Area in 5 mm squares	Area in cm²
1	156	25	6.25
2	123	20	4.91
3	314	50	12.57
4	157	25	6.27
5	109	17	4.36
6	47	26	1.89
7	66	11	2.65
8	79	13	3.14
9	146	23	5.85
10	134	21	5.35
11	94	15	3.75
12	39	6	1.58
13	10	2	0.39
14	5	1	0.20
15	177	28	7.07
16	49	8	1.95
17	14	2	0.58
18	56	9	2.25
19	28	5	1.13
20	65	10	2.60
21	139	22	5.56
22	120	19	4.78
23	73	12	2.92
24	73	12	2.92
25	43	7	1.72
26	25	4	1.00
27	98	16	3.91
28	79	13	3.14
29	491	79	19.63
30	20	3	0.79
32	11	2	0.43
33	146	23	5.83
35	44	7	1.77
36	135	22	5.41
37	81	13	3.23
38	24	4	0.97
40	43	7	1.73

Grid Sheet 5 mm

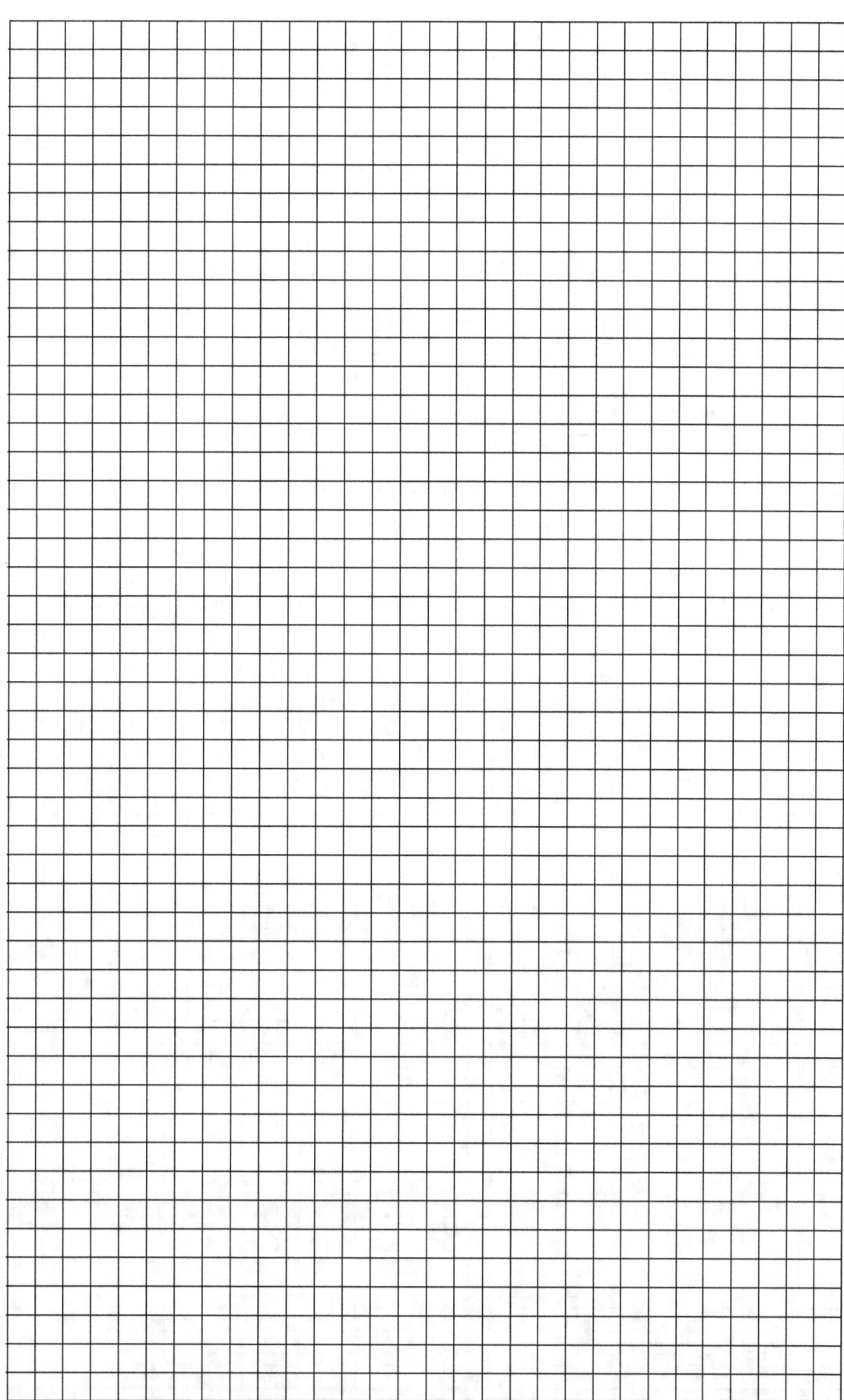

Grid Sheet 2 mm

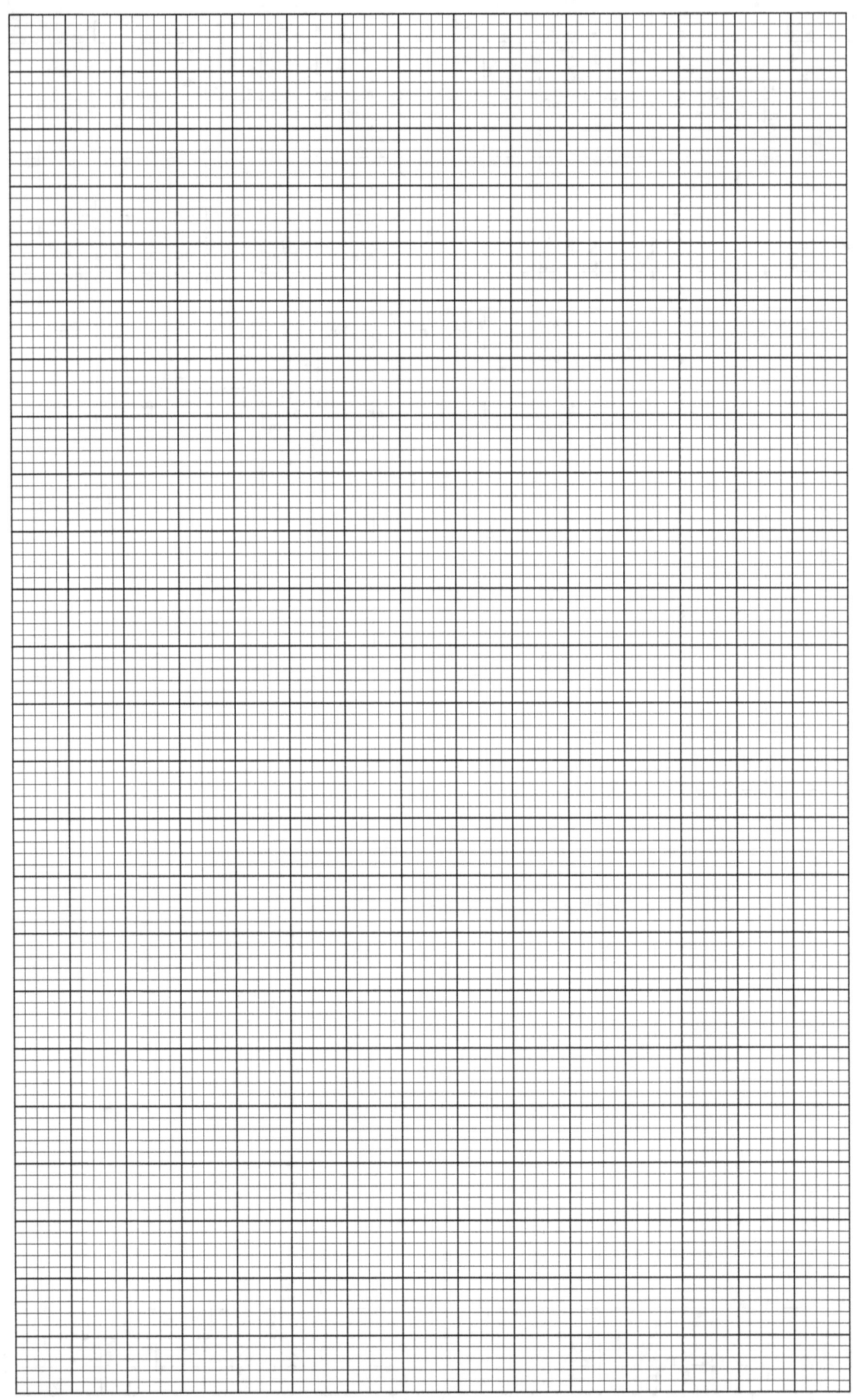

LESSON 7

Straight Line Curves

Years 5 to 9

Constructing Envelopes of Curves

This lesson involves students using the number line on their MATHOMAT to construct envelopes for the parabola and, in the higher year levels, the ellipse and hyperbola. Students specify the 'rules' for drawing the straight lines in terms of either numeric or algebraic relationships.

In this lesson students will:

- use geometric instruments to make accurate constructions;

- construct envelopes of curves;

- identify various curves and investigate their properties; and

- devise rules to specify relationships in either numeric or algebraic form.

Materials Required

For each student:

- a MATHOMAT;
- unlined paper (scrap paper will do); and
- well sharpened pencils.

Lesson Summary

- Constructing the envelope of a parabola by joining points on perpendicular straight lines;
- investigating the effect of changing the angle of intersection of the lines;
- devising a numeric or algebraic 'rule' for joining the points;
- constructing envelopes of circles by joining evenly spaced points on a circle;
- investigating envelopes of other curves produced by joining points circles, intersecting and parallel lines; and
- (optional) creating patterns by joining points on a circle

For the Teacher

We usually think of a curve as being the *locus* of its set of points—i.e. the set of points which lie on the curve.

However, we can also think of a curve as being produced by its *envelope*—i.e. the set of lines which are tangent to the curve at each point. Of course we can't draw all the lines in the envelope—if we could we would get a solid black region representing the area 'outside' the curve.

In this lesson, students use the number lines on their MATHOMAT to join points on pairs of intersecting lines according to different rules to produce envelopes for the parabola and, in higher year levels, the ellipse and hyperbola. The rules for these constructions can be specified using either numeric or algebraic relationships.

The MATHOMAT template contains several circles with evenly spaced markings on their circumferences. For example, circle 29 has 100 evenly spaced marks on its circumference. This circle can therefore also be used to produce 50, 25, 20, 10, 5, 4 or 2 evenly spaced points. Similarly, circle 3, which has 60 evenly spaced marks on its circumference, can also be marked with 30, 20, 15, 12, 10, 6, 5, 4, 3 or 2 evenly spaced points.

This lesson also asks students to join points on their MATHOMAT circles using different rules in order to produce envelopes of the circle and the cardioid.

As an optional conclusion to the lesson, students can create patterns by joining points on the circumference of a circle using arcs of the same circle instead of straight lines.

Encourage students to use sharp pencils in order to construct figures as accurately as possible. (Pencils are preferable to pens in this lesson as incorrect lines can be more easily erased if necessary.)

Lesson Outline

1. Constructing the envelope of a parabola using perpendicular lines

Ask students to draw perpendicular lines as shown below and use their MATHOMAT number line to mark off unit intervals from 0 to 7. (For quick ways to construct perpendicular lines, see page 2 of the MATHOMAT Instruction Book.)

Students can then use straight lines to join points on the horizontal and vertical lines, joining point 7 to point 1, point 6 to point 2, etc, as shown here.

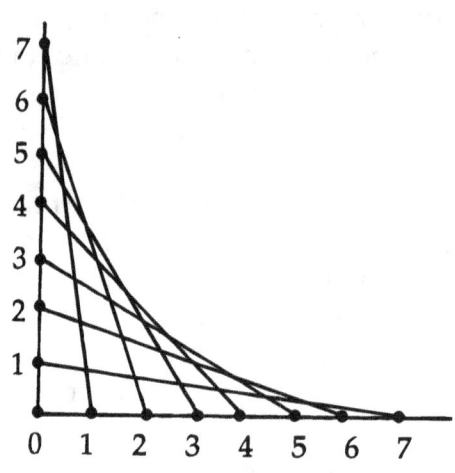

Discuss with students the 'shape' formed by the straight lines—the 'white part' looks like a curve. Explain that this session is mainly about producing curves in this way—i.e. by producing what is called an envelope of the curve. With older students, you may wish to introduce the term tangent, at least intuitively, by pointing out that the straight lines 'touch' the curve but never cut it.

2. Investigating the effect of changing the angle of intersection

Ask students to work individually or in groups to investigate the effect of changing the angle of intersection of the lines on the curve produced—continue to use the same rule of joining points 7 and 1, etc, at this stage.

Students should be given the opportunity to discuss their drawings in order to establish that, no matter what angle is used, the curve obtained is still similar in many ways to the one produced in part 1 above—for example, the diagram below illustrates the case when the lines intersect at 30°.

In each case, the curve produced is part of a parabola. Among similarities students should notice, is the fact that each curve is symmetrical about a line which bisects the angle formed by the pair of intersecting lines. The term parabola can be introduced here—perhaps with a few other examples drawn on the board—as it will be useful to have names for the various curves drawn.

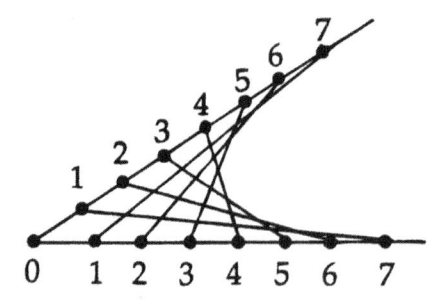

3. Devising a rule for joining the points

Ask students to devise a rule to use when joining the points. Explain that they may need such a rule, if, for example, they wanted to tell a friend over the telephone how to reproduce their curve.

After students have spent a few minutes devising and writing down their rule, hold a brief class discussion where students share the different rules obtained.

Depending on the year level, possible answers might include:

'The two numbers used always add to 8.'

'Join the point x to the point (8 – x).'

4. Circles within circles

Ask students to work individually or in groups to investigate the effect of joining evenly spaced points on the circumference of a circle.

Suggest that students begin by drawing either circle 3 or circle 29 from their MATHOMAT and marking a chosen number of equally spaced points on the circumference. This involves careful counting, marking and numbering of the appropriate MATHOMAT points. (Initially younger students could be encouraged to use circle 29 with 10 or 20 points.)

Students can then join designated points on the circumference of their circle, as illustrated here.
In this example, the figure was produced using circle 29, with 20 evenly spaced points as marked. Each point x was then joined to the point x + 3 (i.e. point 1 was joined to point 4, point 2 joined to point 5, etc). Note that point 18 is joined to 'point 21', which doesn't exist but is in fact understood to be point 1.

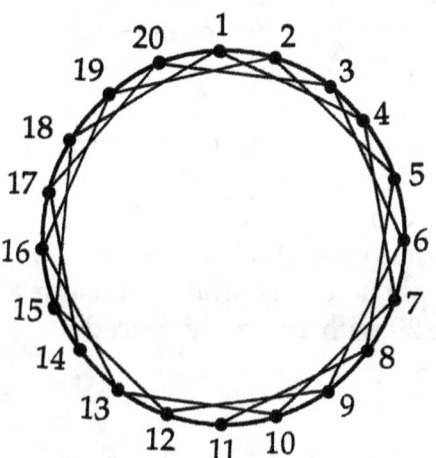

Depending on the year level,
instructions for joining points using the MATHOMAT straight edge can be given in many different ways. For
example, students might give instructions such as those listed below:

'Label the points from 1 to 20, in order. Now join one point to the point three away from it, and the next point to the one three from it, and so on.'

'Label the points from 1 to 20, in order. Join point 1 to point 4, point 2 to point 5, point 3 to point 6, etc.'

'Label the points from 1 to 20, in order. Join the point x to the point x + 3, except that when you get a number greater than 20 you will need to subtract 20 from the answer.'

The diagram below was produced using the same circle with the same spacing, but this time joining point x to point x + 5.

After each student has produced one drawing, discuss as a class the effects of :

- varying the number of points on the circumference; and

- varying the value of 'c' when we join point x to point x + c (as happened above where in the first example we used c = 3 while in the second example we used c = 5).

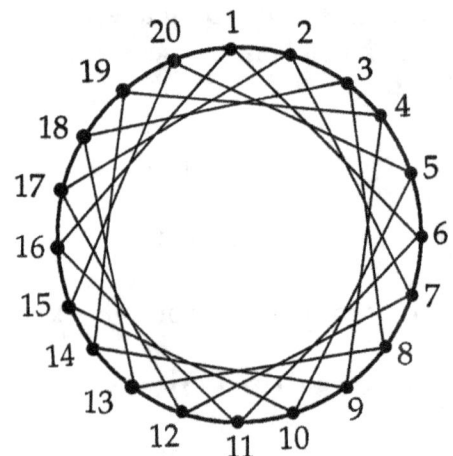

(Of course you would not necessarily use this type of language with students!)

5. Other curves

Several other well-known families of curves can be obtained by joining points on the circumference of a circle or on parallel or intersecting straight lines.

For example, the heart-shaped *cardioid* can be obtained by joining the point x to the point 2x on the circumference of a circle—the example here was produced using circle 29 with 20 evenly spaced points.

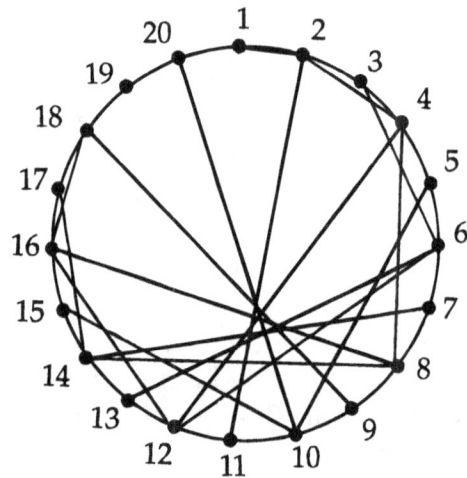

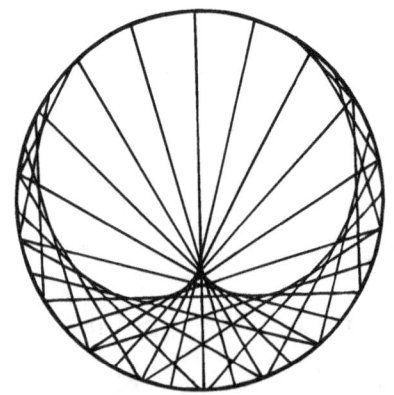

The cardioid can be seen more clearly on the second example shown here, which is based on 32 evenly spaced points.

A *hyperbola* can be obtained by joining a point x to the point c/x on perpendicular lines. The example below shows some of the lines obtained when c = 24.

The lines shown were obtained by choosing pairs of points so that their product is 24 (e.g. the point 12 is joined to the point 2, while the point 3 is joined to the point 8). Other lines can be added by estimating the fractional points on the number lines.

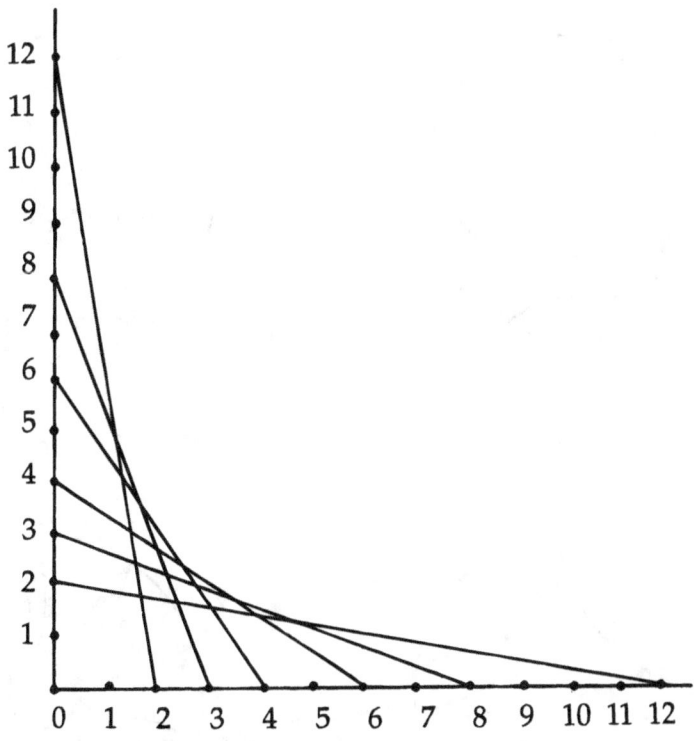

The envelope of an *ellipse* can be obtained by using parallel lines and joining the point x to the point $1/x$, as shown here. For example, the point 4 is joined to the point $1/4$, while the point -2 is joined to the point $-1/2$.

Ask students to produce the envelopes of one or more of these curves, using the instructions given above.

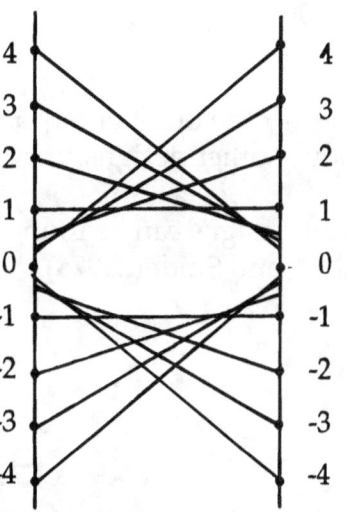

6. (Optional) creating patterns using arcs of circles

Ask students to draw additional circles and mark up to 10 evenly spaced points on their circumference. They can then join selected points using circular arcs (from the same circle) by positioning the MATHOMAT circle template over the chosen points. Some possible results are shown below:

Circle 3, using six points

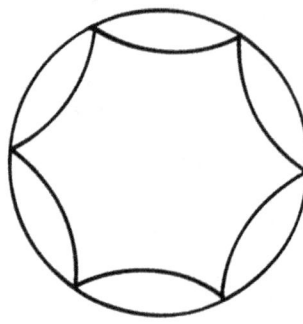

Circle 29, using four points

Circle 29, using ten points

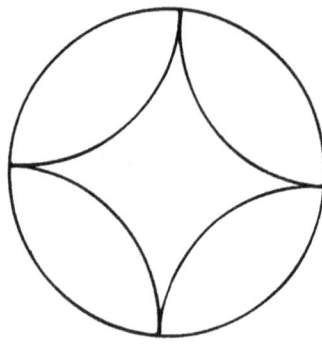

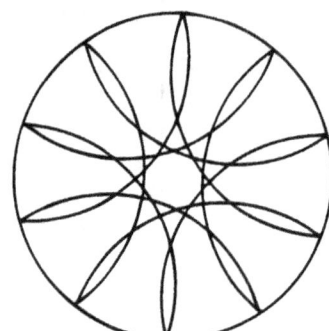

Students can vary the number of points and the rules for joining them in order to produce other designs.

Other ideas for designs can be found in books such as Phillips (1996) and Seymour, Silvey and Snider (1974).

References

Phillips, G. (1996). *GeoMat Investigations*. Croydon North, Vic: Geoff Phillips Publications.

Seymour, D., Silvey, L. & Snider, J. (1994). *Line Designs* Palo Alto, CA: Creative Publications.

LESSON 8

Where Are We?

Years 6 to 9

Maps, Bearings and Distances

This lesson introduces students to the cardinal point and the more precise 360 degree methods of specifying bearings on maps. The lesson includes problems and activities that involve measuring and calculating distances using map scales.

In this lesson students will:

- specify bearings using the compass rose and in degrees;
- calculate distances represented on a map, using the map scale;
- measure bearings with a protractor; and
- use bearings to find the perimeter of a block of land.

Materials Required

For each student:

- a MATHOMAT;
- unlined paper (scrap paper will do);
- a fine-point pen or pencil;
- a copy of Worksheets 8.2, 8.3 and 8.4 (photocopy masters are provided at the end of the lesson);
- felt-tipped and highlighter pens; and
- a drawing pin with their initials marked on it.

Additional materials:

- a piece of chalk for each group of four students;
- at least one magnetic compass, preferably one for each group of four students (orienteering style compasses similar to those manufactured by Silva or Suunto are ideal);
- a photocopy of Worksheet 8.1, Distances and Bearing of Students Homes from School;
- a street directory or other map of the local area—see the later section For The Teacher for details; and
- (optional) an aerial photograph of the school and its environs.

Lesson Summary

- Marking sites on a map and measuring distances and bearings;
- specifying bearings using the cardinal point and the 360° bearing methods; and
- using bearings and scale diagrams in a surveying exercise.

For the Teacher

The magnetic compass was invented in China about 3000 years ago and reached Europe about 1200 AD. It is a piece of technology still widely used and whose essential method of operation has not changed in all that time!

Modern maps (including road maps and street directories) and compasses simplify the task of finding our way between and within towns and cities, as well as in more remote areas. Any map is an interpretation or representation of part of the earth—just how much of the earth is represented depends on the scale of the map.

In this lesson students identify familiar locations on a map and measure distances and bearings associated with these locations. They use the cardinal point method for referring to bearings when precision is not required, and use the protractor on the MATHOMAT to measure bearings in degrees in situations requiring greater precision. As an example of an application of scales and bearings, students use scale diagrams to calculate perimeters of irregularly shaped blocks of land.

Ideally, the class should be divided into groups of four to six students for this lesson.

To use a map to find our direction of travel we need to know which direction is north on the map—most maps are printed with north at the top. You can use a compass to find the actual direction of north 'on the ground.' In most places there is a difference between magnetic north and true north but, at this introductory level, the difference does not affect the activities in the lesson.

In this lesson, students will need to refer to a map of the local area. Suitable maps can often be constructed from street directories. Select the page of the directory which contains the school, and the pages covering the surrounding areas which contain the homes (H) of most of the students. Join photocopies of these pages to form a map with the school (S) at the approximate centre—typically, nine to twelve pages form a convenient map.

Map constructed from 9 directory pages

		H
H	H	H
	S	H
H	H	H
		H

If your student's homes are widely dispersed then you may need to add further pages to the map, or use a topographical map covering a larger area. Avoid maps with scales less than 1: 50 000.

(In Victoria, a large range of maps and aerial photographs is available from Information Victoria, 356 Collins Street, Melbourne.)

Fasten the map to a notice board and pin a copy of Worksheet 8.1 next to it. If possible, display several copies of the map around the classroom and organise the class into groups of four to six pupils.

Activities in parts 3 and 4 of the lesson are best attempted in a paved area of the school grounds.

Although this is presented as a single lesson, several sessions will be required to complete all the activities.

Lesson Outline

1. Using maps, identifying features and measuring distances

This activity capitalises on the students' knowledge of the local area in order to extend their abilities to use a map, identify significant features on it and measure distances related to these features.

Begin the lesson with a class discussion based on the map of the local area (see For the Teacher). Focus initial discussion on the identification of major roads and significant local features such as parks, streams, sporting venues, etc—use felt-tipped pens of various colours to highlight the features.

Ask students to identify the streets in which they live and indicate the position of their homes with a drawing pin on which they have written their initials. Four or five students working at the map at any one time is sufficient.

If an aerial photograph of the area is available, it will enhance interest in the lesson as well as aid the identification of features.

Hold a class discussion about the information the students have marked on the map—identify clusters of students' homes, the students living closest/ furthest from school, the position of pupils' homes in relation to shops etc . Select some students to demonstrate their routes to school, using highlighter pens to mark the routes.

Ask all students to measure, in centimetres, the straight line length from home to school and the length of the actual route travelled to school. A centimetre scale is provided on the left-hand side of MATHOMAT—the fact that it is transparent is useful when measuring on a map.

Each student can then record their results on a displayed class copy of Worksheet 8.1, as shown below. These lengths should be recorded in the second and fourth columns of the worksheet—the remaining columns will be completed later in the lesson.

Name	Straight line distance to school		Straight line distance to school		Bearing from school to home
	cm	m	cm	m	
Bill	15		21		
Betty	6		9		

2. Calculating distances from map measurements

Begin this part of the lesson with a class discussion of 'scale'. At this stage there is no need to mention map scales as ratios. For example, many street directories have a scale of 1 : 20 000, but discussion should be based on the distance represented by 1 centimetre—in this example, 1 centimetre represents 200 metres.

Topographical maps often have scales with 1 cm representing 250 m or 1 cm representing 500 m.

Initially estimations of distances, rather than exact measurements, are appropriate. If you are using a street directory with a scale of 1 : 20 000, such as Melway, suitable questions for class discussion include:

- How far is it across one page of the street directory?
  (About 20 cm; 4000 m or 4 km.)

- What distance is represented by the length of the page?
  (About 25 cm; 5000 m or 5 km.)

- What is the distance on one side of the grid printed on the page?
  (2 cm; 400 m)

The answers to these questions help students to estimate distances on the class map.

Now ask students to estimate the distances between some of the features previously identified.

Guide discussion to the more accurate calculation of distances using the map scale.

Ask students to calculate the distances to their homes and enter them in the table as shown below. In this example the distances are given in metres. Depending on the age and background of your students you may elect to convert these to kilometres.

Map distances, using a '1 cm represents 200 m' scale, entered on Worksheet 8.1

Name	Straight line distance to school		Length of route to school		Bearing from school to home
	cm	m	cm	m	
Bill	15	3000	21	4200	
Betty	6	1200	9	1800	

(This information is ideal for entering into a spread-sheet. Sorting and graphing exercises can be based on it, and extra columns for the distance travelled each week and for a whole year can be added.)

3. Specifying bearings using a compass rose

Shape 15 on the MATHOMAT is a compass rose. The cardinal points, N, S, E, W, SE, SW, etc are used in situations where precise bearings are not required. For example, a knowledge of them is useful in discussion situations, such as, 'I will meet you on the south west corner', 'Braeside is south east of Melbourne' and 'The south bank of the Yarra.'

To find the bearing (direction) of a feature from the school, place the MATHOMAT compass rose on the map, with the school at its centre and N on the rose aligned with north on the map—the bearing is the cardinal point on the rose closest to the feature. For example, in the diagram below, Bill's home is north east of the school.

The two activities in this part of the lesson clarify the concept of 'bearing' and provide an introduction to its more precise measurement.

Bill's home is NE of the school; the school is SE of Bill's home

Copyright Melway Publishing Pty. Ltd. Reproduced from *Melway Street Directory*, Edition 26, with permission

Begin with a class discussion of N, S, E and W and how these relate to the class map—mark them on the map. Demonstrate the compass rose and ask students to find the bearings (cardinal point) of several features on the map, including their homes, from school. The bearings to homes can be entered in the table.

Name	Straight line distance to school		Length of route to school		Bearing from school to home
	cm	m	cm	m	
Bill	15	3000	21	4200	NE
Betty	9	1200	9	1800	SW

In part 1 of this lesson significant features such as clusters of students' homes were identified. Use the now-completed worksheet to revisit the discussion of these features, incorporating information from the worksheet—for example, 'there is a cluster of four homes about 4000 metres east of the school'.

4. Introducing the magnetic compass

Many students are unable to indicate north in their surroundings. They need the opportunity to relate 'north' as the top of the map, to 'north' as a direction.

Demonstrate a magnetic compass and explain how to use it to find north. If possible, allow each student an opportunity to play with the compass. The N of the compass rose on the MATHOMAT can be oriented so that it points north—the other cardinal points then begin to make sense.

Remind students who confuse east and west of the map of Australia and that Western Australia is 'on the left'.

Organise the class into groups of four and move into the school grounds, preferably onto a paved area. Ask each group to use chalk to mark a north-south line on the ground, using a compass as an aid. Use this to draw an enlarged (1 metre diameter) chalk version of the MATHOMAT compass rose. (This in itself is an interesting exercise. How can the cardinal points be marked reasonably accurately? Why not have a compass rose professionally painted in the school yard?)

Students can now use their large compass roses to find bearings. To find the bearing to an item, students stand in the compass rose and face the item—the bearing is the cardinal point in front of them.

Ask the students to note the bearings of several features visible from the school grounds. The compass roses can be used in part 5 of this lesson.

5. Measuring bearings with a protractor

Bearings measured in degrees are used for surveying and precise navigation. Most modern compasses are marked in degrees from 0° to 360°. By convention, bearings are measured clockwise from north.

Direction	Bearing
North	0°
East	90°
South	180°
West	270°

Ask students to extend the above table by calculating bearings, in degrees, corresponding to additional cardinal points: NNE, NE, ENE, ESE, SE, SSE, SSW, SW, WSW, WNW, NW and NNW. Depending on the space available, some of these can be written on the compass roses drawn in the school grounds.

Students need to be given the opportunity to measure angles on maps which represent bearings—examples given to them must encompass the full range of bearings from 0° to 360°. Demonstrate the measuring of bearings with a protractor, stressing the significance of the N-S line.

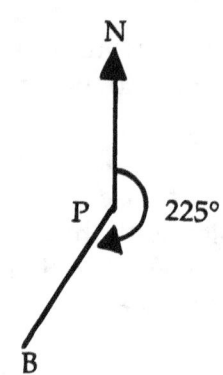
The bearing from P to B is 225°

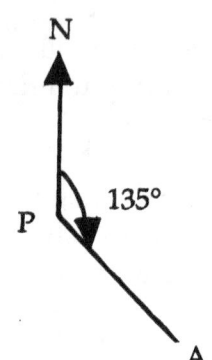
The bearing from P to A is 135°

To measure bearings, turn the MATHOMAT upside down and align 0° on the protractor with north on the map. Although now 'back to front' the protractor scale is still easy to use.

Ask students to complete Worksheets 8.2 and 8.3.

6. Using bearings to find the perimeter of a block of land

The 'radiation' method, which is explained below, may be used to find the perimeter of an irregularly shaped (polygonal) portion of land—it can be used even if the perimeter is not directly measurable because of obstructions etc.

Demonstrate and discuss this technique with the students and ask them to complete one or more of the exercises on Worksheet 8.4.

To use this method, choose an arbitrary point P near the centre of the land. For each corner of the land make two measurements:

- the bearing from point P to the corner; and
- the distance from point P to the corner.

These measurements are now incorporated into a scale diagram—a realistic scale for this example is to use 0.1 cm to represent 1 m.

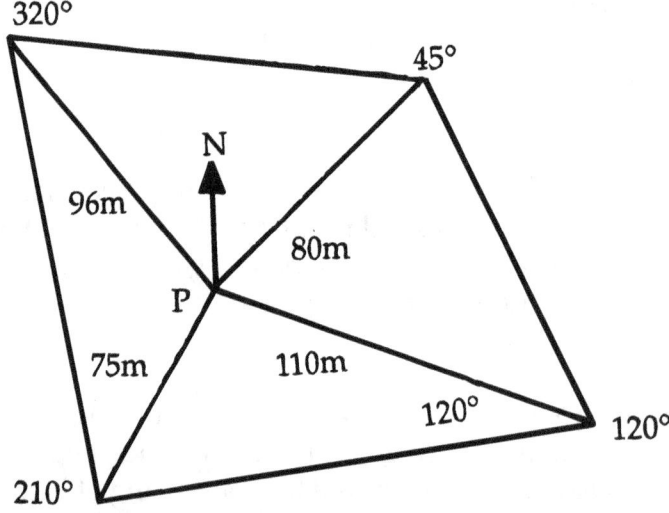

A block of land with corners at A, B, C and D: Bearings and distances are displayed

To construct the diagram draw a N-S line through the central point P and use the protractor on the MATHOMAT to draw lines with the appropriate bearings. By measuring along these lines the corners can be marked and the boundary drawn and measured in centimetres. To calculate the perimeter, measure its length in centimetres and use the same scale to convert this length to metres.

7. Optional extension for older students

An interesting exercise is for students to use the radiation method to find the perimeter of an irregularly shaped section of the school ground.

Mark the corners of the chosen section with school bags or pieces of wood and ask students to measure the distances and bearings from a marked point within the area.

Students will find the measurement of bearings challenging and may require assistance. Two methods are available,

- either, measure the bearings directly with a compass;
- or, draw 'sighting lines' and north-south lines on the ground and measure bearings with a protractor (a 'sighting line' is a line drawn from the fixed point in the direction of the corner).

Compare the calculated perimeter with that found by direct measurement.

Distances and Bearings of Students' Homes from School

Name	Straight line distance to school		Length of route to school		Bearing from school to home
	cm	m	cm	m	

Measuring Bearings in Degrees

Here is a road map of an area south of Melbourne, it includes part of Albert Park Lake. Locate each site in the following list on the map and use the protractor on MATHOMAT to find its bearing, in degrees, from the southern tip of Gunn Island—the island near the north end of the lake.

1. The corner of Queens Rd. and Arthur Street
   (K5) ☐ degrees

2. The Town Hall in Bank Street
   (E2) ☐ degrees

3. Chinese Joss House in Raglan Street
   (E4) ☐ degrees

4. The water fountain in Albert Park Lake

5. The southern end of Dodd Street

6. Palmerston Place

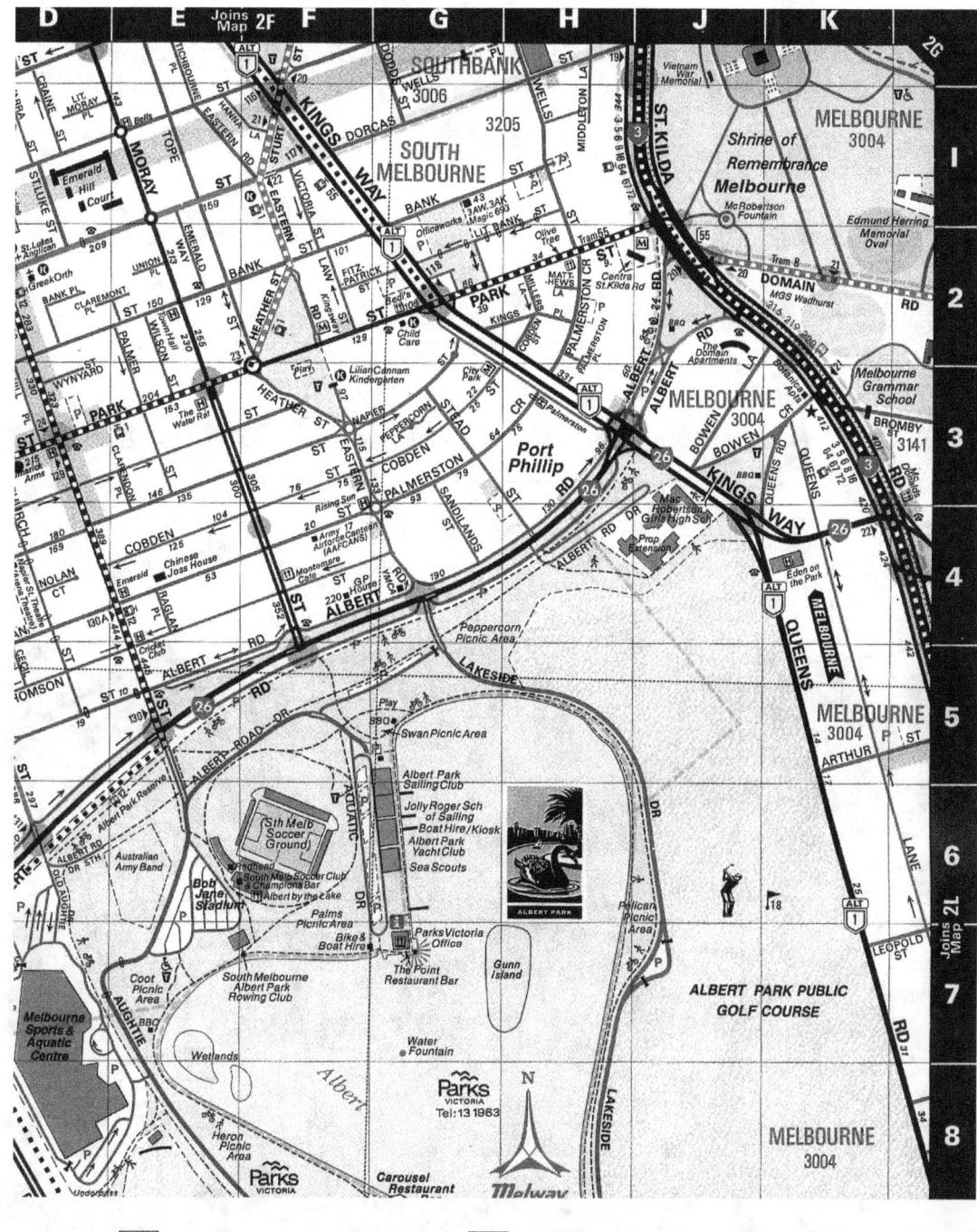

(G7) ☐ degrees   (G1) ☐ degrees   (H2) ☐ degrees

Copyright Melway Publishing Pty. Ltd. Reproduced from *Melway Street Directory* Edition 26, with permission.

WORKSHEET 8.2

MATHS WITH MATHOMAT

75

Find the Surf Beach

To challenge visiting friends one wet day during their holidays, Con and Sue planned complex instructions for a route from home to their favourite surfing beach. Their friends accepted the challenge and, armed with a MATHOMAT and a copy of the map (scale 1cm represents 200 m), successfully followed the directions—they located the correct place on the map. Can you find the surf beach?

The Directions.

Start at Con and Sue's home at the southern end of Woodlands Drive (D3). Follow a bearing of 98° for 400m. Travel due south for 300 m until you reach a road. Follow this road in a generally southern direction for 460 m and turn into the street which has a bearing of 234°. Follow this street for 440 m. Turn into the road which has a bearing of 100° and follow it for just 70 m and turn south. Cross the park to the exit whose bearing is 196° from where you entered the park. Walk south for 40 m then turn onto the road which has a

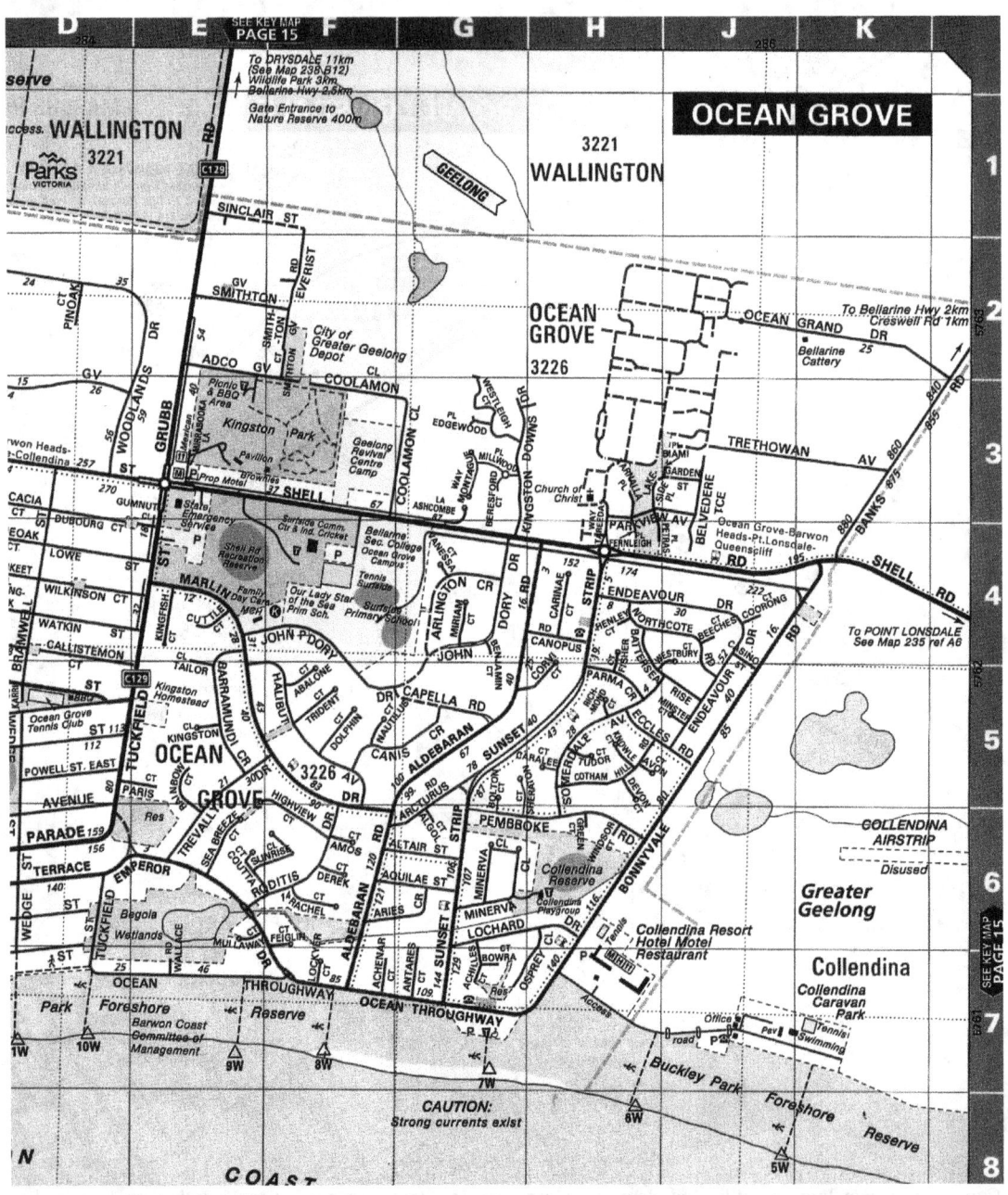

bearing of 93°. Follow this road for 970 m. Travel on a bearing of 180° for 170 m to the meeting place on the beach.

Scale Diagrams and Perimeters

Each of the following is a rough 'field' sketch, made by a surveyor, of a plot of land. Make an accurate scale drawing of each region and find its perimeter.

1.

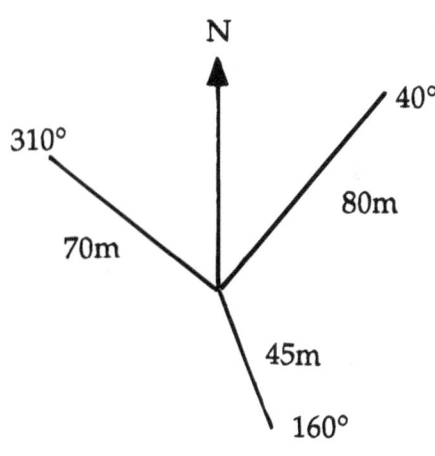

2.

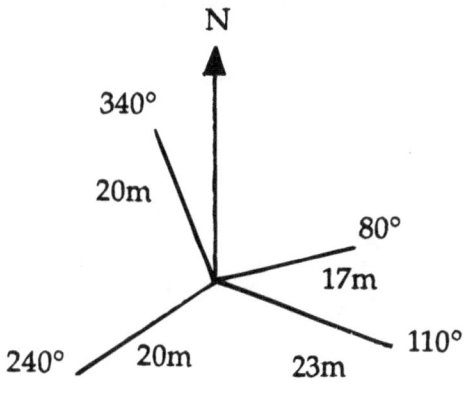

3.

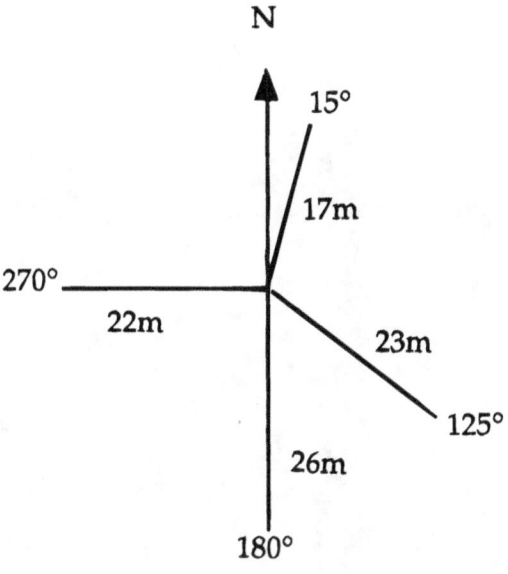

4.

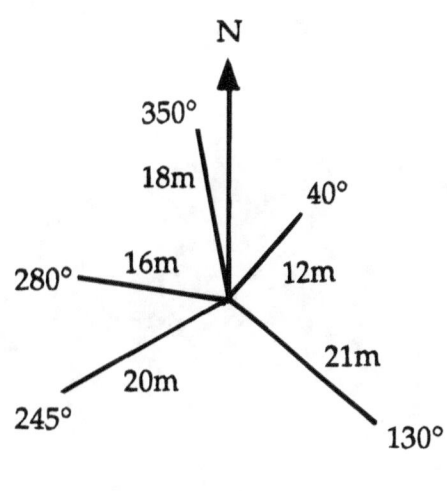

LESSON 9

Round and Round the Circle

Years 4 to 8

Rotational Symmetry

This lesson involves students in investigating rotational symmetry of various MATHOMAT and other shapes and using MATHOMAT shapes to create two-dimensional shapes and patterns with rotational symmetry.

In this lesson students will:

- investigate rotational symmetry in two-dimensional shapes.

Materials Required

For each student:

- a MATHOMAT;

- unlined paper (scrap paper will do);

- a copy of the Worksheet 9.1, Rotational Symmetry in Complex Shapes (a photocopy master is provided at the end of this lesson);

- fine-point pens or pencils; and

- scissors.

Additional materials:

- one overhead projector version or photocopies for each group of students of Transparency 5.1, Lines of Symmetry which was used in Lesson 5.

Lesson Summary

- Identifying rotational symmetry in MATHOMAT shapes;

- classifying shapes according to the number of rotational symmetries;

- completing and constructing two-dimensional shapes and patterns with rotational symmetry;

- identifying rotational symmetry in more complex shapes; and

- (optional) having a brief discussion on the finite symmetry groups of two-dimensional figures.

For the Teacher

This lesson is an extension of Lesson 5, for older students, who may be interested in knowing more about *symmetries*. Students should have completed Lesson 5 before doing this lesson.

A *symmetry* of an object permutes its points while reproducing the same shape exactly. As well as using lines of symmetry to produce reflections, the only other transformations which can be used to transform a *finite two-dimensional* figure into itself are rotations.

Some of the figures on Transparency 5.1, Lines of Symmetry, which was used in Lesson 5 have one or more rotational symmetries. This sheet can either be reproduced on an overhead projector transparency for class discussion or photo-copied for groups of students to look at and discuss.

A regular pentagon, for example, has 10 possible symmetries—five reflections and the five rotations about its centre through 72°, 144° (= 2 x 72°), 216° (= 3 x 72°), 288° (= 4 x 72°), and 0° (which, although it leaves the pentagon 'unchanged' is still counted as a rotation).

In a similar way, any regular polygon with n sides has 2n symmetries—n reflections and n rotations. So, for example, a square has 2 x 4 = 8 symmetries—4 reflections and 4 rotations, while a regular dodecagon (12 sides) has 2 x 12 = 24 symmetries—12 rotations and 12 reflections.

A circle, of course, has infinitely many reflections and rotations.

The full set of symmetries of an object form what is called its *symmetry group*. It turns out that every *finite two-dimensional* figure, apart from the circle—which should perhaps not be considered as finite here—has a symmetry group which consists of either n rotations only or n reflections together with n rotations, where n is some natural number. (Motivated maths students in the upper years may wish to know that the symmetry group consisting of n rotations is *called the cyclic group of order n*, written C_n—because it 'goes round in a cycle' and comes back to the start—while the symmetry group consisting of n reflections and n rotations is called the dihedral group of order 2n, written D_n—because it includes the reflections and so is 'two-faced').

This lesson follows a similar format to Lesson 5.

The lesson provides opportunities for students to explore the rotational symmetries of the MATHOMAT shapes and classify them according to the number of rotational symmetries. For some shapes, students can use the markings on the perimeter to locate the 'centre' and use the protractor to determine the angle of rotation.

The MATHOMAT shapes and curves include those which only have one rotational symmetry, the 'trivial' rotation through 0° (these are the non-half dodecagon); those which have two rotational symmetries, the rotations through 0° and 180° (the ellipses and the non-square parallelograms); those which have three, four, five, six or eight rotational symmetries (the regular polygons with the corresponding number of sides); and the circles, which have infinitely many rotational symmetries.

Depending on the year level, students should be encouraged to attempt to describe their results from the classification activity in general terms like those given above. This can again, as in Lesson 5, form the basis for a valuable class discussion. In the case of the regular polygons, older students should be encouraged to explore the relationship between the number of sides, the number of rotations and the angles of rotation—i.e. the fact that the rotations for an n-sided regular polygon are always through angles which are multiples of $(360/n)°$.

Following the classification activity, students can use their MATHOMAT to construct and create attractive shapes and patterns with rotational symmetry, as well as identify rotational symmetries in more complex patterns.

For older students who are interested, the lesson can conclude with a discussion of the fact that the only finite symmetry groups of two-dimensional figures are C_n and D_n (see above). They can then go back and label each shape with its symmetry group, which then allows them to 'see' and recognise at a glance the types of symmetries.

Symmetry groups of three-dimensional objects have proved a powerful tool in crystallography, as well as playing a key role in modern theoretical physics. For example, a current first year university physics text (Ohanian, 1989) includes a section discussing not only three-dimensional symmetry but also an analysis of the repetitions in the (two-dimensional) work of M. C. Escher—see also Lesson 2 here. It states that

> the repetitive pattern of behavior of the atoms listed in the Periodic Table ... can be traced to an underlying symmetry of the equations governing the motion of the electrons in the atoms. And the regular pattern of the behavior of the elementary particles in 'families' of particles ... can be traced to a symmetry of the parameters describing the internal structure of these particles. Such abstract mathematical symmetries play a key role in physics. In fact, much of modern theoretical physics can be described as a search for symmetry. (p. I-1)

Lesson Outline

1. Introducing rotational symmetry

Use an overhead projector transparency or photocopy of Transparency 5.1, Lines of Symmetry to introduce a class discussion about rotational symmetry.

The four examples on the sheet include two figures, the mask and the Balmain Bug, which can only be reproduced by rotations through 0° (or other multiples of 360°)—i.e. they have only one rotational symmetry, the 'trivial' rotation.

The top right hand figure, however, has three rotational symmetries—the rotations about its 'centre' through 0°, 120° and 240°. This can be demonstrated on the overhead projector by reproducing the figure on an overhead transparency, cutting it out roughly, placing a mark of some kind at the top, and rotating it while asking students to say stop when it 'looks the same as at the start', ignoring the mark for the moment. This can be repeated until it 'returns to its original position' after three such rotations—the fact that it has returned to its original position is shown by the mark being again at the top. Alternatively, groups of students could cut out the figure and do this at their desks.

It is important to realise that the rotation must be about the centre of the figure. When working at their desks, students might wish to 'pin down' their figures at the centre with the point of a ball point pen.

Note that we usually disregard the fact that rotations of 480° (= 120° + 360°) or 840° (= 120° + 2 x 360°), etc, would have the same effect as a rotation through 120°.

Through class discussion or by working in groups, students can now discover that the bottom left hand figure has twelve rotational symmetries —the rotations through 0°, 30°, 60°, 90° ..., 330°, since 30 = 360/12.

A class discussion can also include a brief investigation of the rotational symmetries of upper case letters of the alphabet—e.g. The letter A has only the trivial rotation through 0°, while N and Z have two rotational symmetries, the rotations through 0° and 180°.

2. Identifying rotational symmetries of the MATHOMAT shapes

Ask students to work individually or in groups to find the rotational symmetries for most of the MATHOMAT shapes and curves—shapes such as 13, 14, 26, 28, 30, 32 and 35, which are small and which are repeated in a larger size should be omitted.

If students work individually, they will need to be allocated shapes to test as they can decide how to share the shapes to be tested—a good way which results in a variety for each student would be to take every fifth shape in a group of five (e.g. the first student gets shapes 1, 6, 11, 18, etc to test, since 13 and 14 are omitted).

Each student can cut out the shapes to be tested and find the number or rotational symmetries for each one as was done in part 1 of this lesson. A good way to do this is to get students to draw the shape they are testing again, superimpose the cut-out shape, mark one vertex and the centre, 'pin down the centre' and rotate the shape until it fits the drawing again. Students can repeat the rotation until the shape returns to its original position, in order to find the number of rotational symmetries.

Students should also be encouraged to find the angles of rotation, either by measurement or by calculation. With experience, some students will be able to work out the number of rotations by reasoning such as: A regular pentagon has 5 equal sides and 5 equal angles, so it will have 5 rotational symmetries. In order to return to its original position it must rotate through 360°. So each rotation must be through an angle of $(360/5)° = 72°$.

3. Classifying MATHOMAT shapes according to the number of rotational symmetries

Ask students to work in groups to classify the MATHOMAT shapes according to the number of rotational symmetries.

As in Lesson 5, each group should be encouraged to record and display their results in preparation for a class discussion. Students can complete a table like the one shown on the following page.

Also as in Lesson 5, there are many different ways to produce such a table and students should be encouraged to plan how to display their results.

As soon as most groups have completed their recordings or displays, hold a class discussion to compare results and attempt to come to agreement on the types of shapes which have different numbers of rotational symmetries. This discussion can be valuable in developing students' ability to use conventional geometric language to describe classes of shapes at all of the year levels suggested for this lesson.

Sample table classifying MATHOMAT shapes according to numbers of rotational symmetries

Number of rotational symmetries	Shapes
1	33, 24
2	6, 21
3	
4	
5	10
6	
8	
∞	35

LESSON 9

MATHS WITH MATHOMAT

85

4. Identifying rotational symmetries in more complex shapes

Ask students to work individually or in groups to complete the Worksheet 9.1, Rotational Symmetry in Complex Shapes.

The first part asks students to find the number of rotational symmetries, while question two asks fo the number of lines of reflection (see Lesson 5).

As before, students need to realise that when they are provided with photos of objects occurring in real life, it is the object not the photo which is being considered and also that real life objects won't be perfectly symmetrical!

5. (Optional) brief discussion of finite symmetry groups of two-dimensional figures

For older students who are interested, this portion of the lesson can conclude with a discussion of the fact that the only finite symmetry groups of two-dimensional figures are C_n and D_n (see For the Teacher). They can then go back and label each of the figures on the Worksheet 9.1, Rotational Symmetry in Complex Shapes with its symmetry group, which then allows them to 'see' and recognise at a glance the types of symmetries.

6. Creating symmetrical patterns

Ask students to create their own patterns with rotational symmetry using their MATHOMAT. Older students can be asked to produce patterns with specified numbers of rotational symmetries and/or lines of reflection. (Note that the number of reflections is always either zero or the same as the number of rotations.)

Reference

Ohanian, H. C. (1989). *Physics* (2nd edn). New York: W. W. Norton.

Rotational Symmetry in Complex Shapes

1. For each of the diagrams below, find the number of rotational symmetries and record your answer in the first space provided (R for rotations).

   a) MATHOMAT

     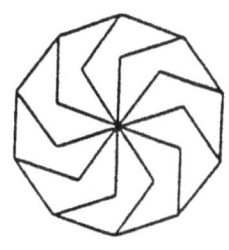

   DESIGNS

    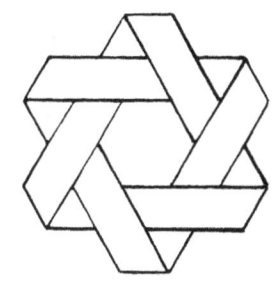 

   ☐ L ☐   R ☐ L ☐   R ☐ L ☐

   R

   b) OTHER DESIGNS

     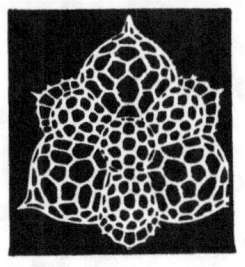

   R ☐ L ☐   R ☐ L ☐   R ☐ L ☐

   b) REAL-LIFE OBJECTS—of course these will not be perfect!

LESSON

10

Stars, Circles and Mystic Signs

Years 4 to 9

Creating Patterns with Circles

This lesson requires students to investigate various figures, including the Mystic Rose and star polygons, which can be formed using equally spaced points on the MATHOMAT circles.

In this lesson students will:

- discover properties of polygons inscribed in a circle;

- select, use and communicate strategies for solving a non-routine problem; and

- use geometrical tools to make accurate drawings.

Materials Required

For each student:

- a MATHOMAT;
- unlined paper (scrap paper will do);
- extra-fine-point pens or very sharp pencils; and
- an eraser.

Additional materials:

- one overhead projector version or one photocopy for each group of students of Handout 10.1, Stars, Circles and Mystic Signs (a photocopy master is included at the end of this lesson); and
- (optional) one overhead projector version or one photocopy for each group of students of Handout 10.2, Other Designs Using Points on Circles (a photocopy master of this is also included).

Lesson Summary

- Identifying the number of equally spaced points on various MATHOMAT circles;
- investigating the number of lines in Mystic Rose patterns for different numbers of points;
- producing star polygons and investigating their properties; and
- (optional) creating other attractive designs using points on a circle.

For the Teacher

In this lesson, students use the equally spaced marks on various MATHOMAT circles to construct and investigate figures such as the Mystic Rose pattern (see Handout 10.1, Stars, Circles and Mystic Signs) and star polygons. In order to choose appropriate circles to create their designs, students will need to begin by finding the number of points marked on the various MATHOMAT circles (refer also to Lesson 7).

The Mystic Rose pattern is produced by marking points at equal intervals on the circumference of a circle and joining each point to every other point. Examples for 5 and 18 points are provided on Handout 10.1, Stars, Circles and Mystic Signs, at the end of this lesson. In this lesson, all students produce a 3 and 4 point Mystic Rose pattern. Depending on their year level and construction skills, each student also produces another Mystic Rose pattern with 5, 6, 8, 10 or 12 points. Students can then investigate the number of lines in a Mystic Rose pattern and attempt to find a way of calculating this number without needing to count. Older students can generalise their results for 100 points, or even for n points, where n is any natural number.

All regular polygons can be inscribed in a circle, with their vertices producing equally spaced points on the circumference. So, for example, the vertices of a regular pentagon form 5 equally spaced points on the circumference of a circle. This means that one way of drawing a regular pentagon is to take 5 equally spaced points on the circumference of a circle and join each point to the 'next' point.

Star polygons are produced by joining every second (or third, or fourth, etc) point. So, for example, the pentagram on Handout 10.1, Stars, Circles and Mystic Signs can be produced by starting with 5 equally spaced points on the circumference of a circle and joining every second point. Similarly, the hexagram on the same sheet can be produced by starting with 6 equally spaced points and joining every second point. In this case (because 2 is a factor of 6) the hexagram will need to be produced using two separate lines, each joining 3 points. Star polygons can easily be identified by using the symbol (n,m) to indicate that they are formed by starting with n equally spaced points and joining every m-th point. So the pentagram has the symbol (5, 2) and the hexagram the symbol (6, 2). Older students can investigate questions such as 'When do two star polygons look the same?' and 'How can we tell in advance how many separate lines will be needed to draw a star polygon?'

Other attractive patterns can also be formed using equally spaced points on a circle. A few of these are illustrated on Handout 10.2, Other Designs Using Points on Circles. Students can copy these or create their own.

An extra-fine-point pen or very sharp pencil is essential for patterns based on a large numbers of points.

Lesson Outline

1. Identifying the number of equally spaced points on MATHOMAT circles

This lesson requires students to use equally spaced points on the various MATHOMAT circles. In order to produce neat designs, it is preferable to use the largest circle possible in each case—therefore of the circles with 4 equally spaced marks (circles 13, 14, 28, 30 and 35) only circle 28 will be used. However, a balance needs to be struck between using larger circles and ones where it is easy to mark the required number of equally spaced points.

Ask students to work in groups or individually to investigate the possible numbers of equally spaced points which can be marked on the various MATHOMAT circles. Each student should complete a table like the one shown below.

Circle number	Number of equally spaced points	Numbers of equally spaced points possible
2	10	2, 5, 10
3	60	2, 3, 4, 5, 6, 10, 12, 15, 20, 30, 60
15	32	2, 4, 8, 16, 32
28	4	2, 4,
29	100	2, 4, 8, 16, 32

2. Drawing the Mystic Rose pattern

The Mystic Rose pattern is produced by marking points at equal intervals on the circumference of a circle and joining each point to every other point. Examples for 5 and 18 points are provided on Handout 10.1, Stars, Circles and Mystic Signs at the end of this lesson. Show the class these on an overhead projector or a photocopy can be provided for each group.

Ask students to produce their own 3 and 4 point Mystic Rose patterns using circle 3. Depending on their year level and construction skills, students should also produce one or more Mystic Rose pattern using 5, 6, 8, 10 or 12 points (using circles 2, 3, 15, 29 or 3 respectively).

It is a good idea to check that students have the correct number of equally spaced points before they start drawing the lines.

3. The Mystic Rose challenge

The challenge for students is to investigate the number of lines in a Mystic Rose pattern—their own and perhaps the ones on Handout 10.1, Stars, Circles and Mystic Signs.

Ask older students to generalise their results for 100 points, or even for n points, where n is any natural number.

For the 3, 4 and 5 point Mystic Rose patterns, it is easy to count the number of lines, but for larger numbers of points students will need to find a way of calculating without counting.

Allow students to find and use their own solution strategies. This is likely to take some time—perhaps the best part of a lesson—but it can lead to a very valuable class discussion afterwards.

At the end of this part of the lesson, ask students to share their solution strategies with the class. Those students who were able to generalise their results to large numbers can explain how they did this. Different strategies can be compared in terms of how easy they are to generalise and how easy they are to explain.

Possible strategies

A number of possible strategies which students might use are illustrated below, using the 8 point Mystic Rose as an example.

Mystic Rose pattern for 8 points

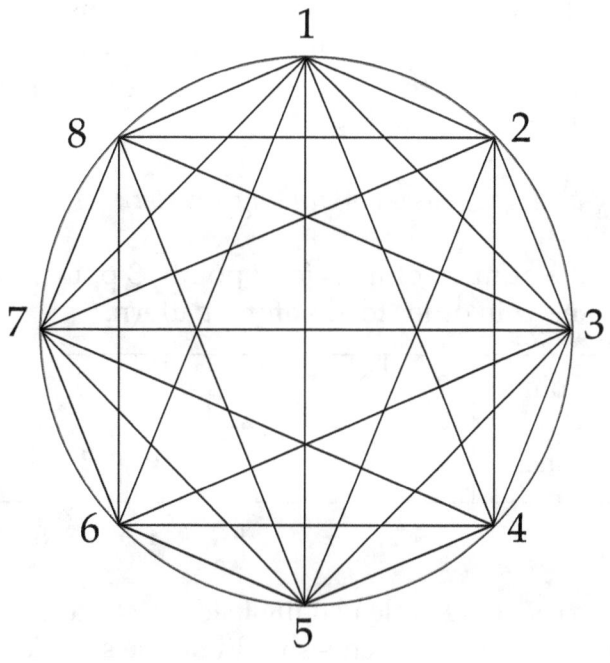

Strategy 1: Counting the number of lines—version 1

Point 1 is joined to 7 other points
Point 2 is joined to 6 other points (not counting point 1)
Point 3 is joined to 5 other points (not counting points 1 & 2)
...
Point 7 is joined to 1 other point
Point 8 is joined to 0 new points
So there are 7 + 6 + 5 + 4 + 3 + 2 + 1 = 28 lines.

While this is a good method, it is rather difficult to generalise to larger numbers of points. However, a positive aspect of using this solution strategy is that it can lead to students finding their own creative ways of adding lists of consecutive numbers. For older students, this can be used as an introduction to arithmetic progressions.

Strategy 2: Counting the number of lines—version 2

Each point is joined to 7 other points, so there are (8 x 7) ÷ 2 = 28 lines. We need to divide by 2 since each line joins two points and, if we just used 8 x 7 = 56, we would count each line twice.

This is a neater method and generalises easily to finding that there are (100 x 99) ÷ 2 = 4950 lines for 100 points and (n x [n–1]) ÷ 2 lines for n points.

Many students, however, start by using this method, but abandon it after finding it gives the wrong answer when they forget to divide by two.

This provides an excellent opportunity for students to find a way to 'check their answers'—it can be quite difficult to persuade students that true checking involves finding some other way to confirm their answer than by 'asking the teacher' or just repeating the arithmetic! This problem can be used to introduce students to the valuable strategy of checking their solution method by testing it on a simpler case.

Strategy 3: Looking at simpler cases and finding a pattern

Students can find the number of lines for 2 points, 3 points, etc, and make a table like the one below in order to look for a pattern.

Number of Points	2	3	4	5	6	7	...
Number of Lines	1	3	6	10	15	21	...

+2 +3 +4 +5 +6 ...

Filling in a few entries of the table usually leads to students finding a pattern. However, it is important that students should not be satisfied with just finding a pattern but should understand the need to find a 'reason why it works'. In this case, each time you add a point it will need to be joined to all the existing points. So, for example, adding the eighth point will add 7 new lines, since it will need to be joined to each of the previous 7 points, and, in general, adding the n-th point will create an extra (n–1) lines.

While looking at simpler cases is a valuable problem solving strategy for students to use, this strategy is again difficult to apply to larger Mystic Rose patterns or use to provide a general answer for the number of lines.

4. Investigating star polygons

The pentagram

All regular polygons can be inscribed in a circle, with their vertices producing equally spaced points on the circumference—for example, the vertices of a regular pentagon form 5 equally spaced points on the circumference of a circle. So one way of drawing a regular pentagon is to take 5 equally spaced points on the circumference of a circle and join each point to the 'next' point.

Ask students to make three copies of circle 29 and mark 5 equally spaced points on each, starting at 'the top'.

Now ask students to draw a pentagon on the first of their circles by joining adjacent points.

Star polygons are produced by joining every second (or third, or fourth, etc) point.

Ask students to use their second copy of circle 29 to produce a star polygon by joining every second point—i.e. by joining the points in the following order: 1 – 3 – 5 – 2 – 4 – 1.

This star polygon is called the *pentagram* and has the symbol (5, 2)—meaning that it was formed by using 5 equally spaced points and joining every second one.

Ask students to use their third circle to draw the star polygon (5, 3)—i.e. the one obtained by joining every third point. Why does it look the same as the pentagram? What would happen if they drew (5, 4)? What would be a good symbol to use for the pentagon?

Students may be interested to know that, during the time of Pythagoras, a secret society or brotherhood called the Pythagoreans took the pentagram as their badge or symbol by which any member was able to immediately recognise a fellow member. The pentagram was also regarded as a symbol of health.

(Optional) ask students to make their own copy of the nested pentagram shown on Handout 10.1, Stars, Circles and Mystic Signs, using their drawing of the star polygon (5, 3)—each new pentagram can easily be produced by joining every second point of the pentagon formed at the 'centre' of the previous one. Of course, in theory, this process can be repeated infinitely!

An amazing property of the infinite set of nested regular pentagrams is that the length of every line segment is in the Golden Ratio to the length of the next smallest segment. This fact was well known to the Pythagoreans.

The hexagram

Ask students to produce the star polygon (6, 2) by using 6 equally spaced points on circle 3. This six-pointed star, which is called the *hexagram*, will probably be familiar to students as the Star of David. Like the pentagram, it was widely used in the past to ward off evil.

Two other ways of producing the hexagram using the MATHOMAT are shown on Handout 10.1, Stars, Circles and Mystic Signs. The first of these methods uses shape 23 to produce two interlocking triangles. Because the lines drawn are relatively thick, it is probably best to draw the hexagram by tracing one of the triangles and positioning the other 'by eye'—using the marks for the mid-points to position the second triangle results in an unbalanced design. The second quick way to draw the hexagram is to draw the hexagon (shape 9) and, working clockwise around it, extend each of the sides sufficiently to form the six-pointed star. Demonstrate these ways to the class.

The 'magic hexagram' on Handout 10.1, Stars, Circles and Mystic Signs was formed by joining the opposite points of a hexagram and numbering all of the points and intersections in a 'magic way'. Challenge students to find its magical properties.

Other star polygons

Ask students to use circle 13 or 24 to investigate star polygons with 10 points. How many different shapes can be produced using star polygons with 10 points? Which star polygons with 10 points look the same? Which star polygons with 10 points need more than one continuous line to produce? How many lines do they need? Why? What is 'different' about the star polygon (10,5)?

Ask older students to make conjectures about star polygons with different numbers of points (e.g. 15, 16, 100, n) without drawing them and attempt to answer general questions such as 'When do two star polygons look the same?', 'How can we tell in advance how many lines will be needed to draw a star polygon?' and 'What other star polygons would look similar to the star polygon (10, 5)?'

5. (Optional) creating designs using polygons in circles

Handout 10.2, Other Designs Using Points on Circles, illustrates a number of attractive designs which can be produced using equally spaced points on a circle.

To complete this lesson, ask students to copy these or create their own designs. A good quality presentation can be achieved by drawing the construction lines with a soft pencil, completing the design with a waterproof pen and finally erasing unwanted construction lines.

Stars, Circles and Mystic Signs

THE MYSTIC ROSE

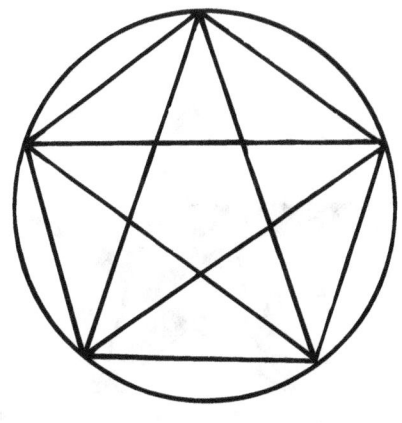

The 5 point Mystic Rose pattern

The 18 point Mystic Rose pattern

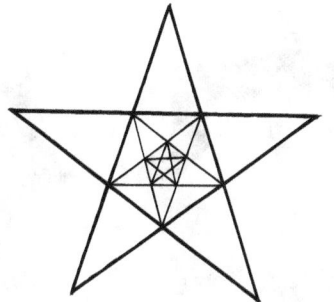

PENTAGRAMS

The pentagram

The hexagram

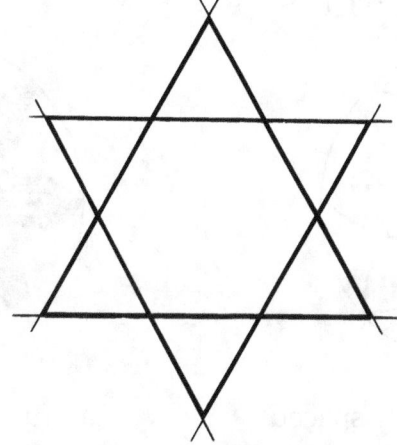

Another way of drawing a hexagram

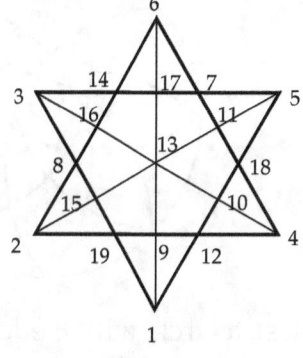

Nested pentagrams
The magic hexagram

Other Designs Using Points on Circles

A DESIGN BASED ON THE PENTAGRAM

Use a circle with 5 equally spaced points to construct a pentagram and join the points as shown.

Carefully erase the circle and shade the regions as shown.

SOME OTHER DESIGNS BASED ON REGULAR POLYGONS

A DESIGN BASED ON CIRCLES

Use a circle with 8 equally spaced points and join every third point with an arc of the circle as shown.

Carefully shade the regions as shown.

LESSON 11

Unwrapping the Circle

Years 9 to 12

Constructing the Sine Graph

This lesson introduces students to the number π and its location on a number line. Students then use the unit circle definition of the sine of an angle to construct a sine graph.

In this lesson students will:

- identify π as a number;
- locate multiples of π on a number line;
- define the sine of an angle; and
- construct the graph of the sine function.

Materials Required

For each student:

- a MATHOMAT;
- a photocopy of Worksheet 11.2, Measuring the Sines of Angles, (a photocopy master is included at the end of this lesson);
- unlined paper (scrap paper will do);
- a fine-point pen or pencil;
- access to a scientific calculator or spreadsheet; and
- graph paper.

Additional materials:

- an overhead projector and coloured pens;
- a photocopy for each group of students of Worksheet 11.1, Estimating π (a photocopy master is included at the end of this lesson);
- a collection of circular objects of various radii (plates, jars, bike wheel, etc); and
- a transparency of each of the diagrams in Transparencies 11.1, 11.2, and 11.3 (a photocopy master is included at the end of this lesson).

Lesson Summary

- Finding approximate value of using circular objects;
- measuring distance around the unit circle;
- using radians to measure angles
- using the MATHOMAT to produce an 'unwrapped' circle;
- defining the sine of an angle;
- drawing the sine graph; and
- estimating the sines of angles.

For the Teacher

Students need a thorough understanding of the number π before they are introduced to the sine function and its graph. Included among students' common misconceptions of the nature of π are that it is 'part of a circle' and 'another way of measuring angles'. It is essential that students understand that π is a number that can be represented on a number line.

The number π has a fascinating history. In the Bible, in the Book of Kings and Chronicles, the value of π is given as 3. Ancient Egyptians used the more accurate value of 3.16—their geometrical investigations were triggered by the regular flooding of agricultural land by the Nile. By 150 AD the value of π was assumed to be 3.1416.

Archimedes, the Greek philosopher and mathematician, was fascinated by π. He devised a method of calculating its value by inscribing and circumscribing polygons about a circle; the area of the circle lies between that of the inscribed and circumscribed hexagons—its perimeter lies between that of the two hexagons.

 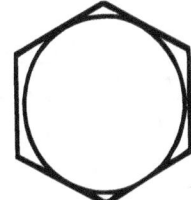

The calculation of the value of π achieved almost cult status and was the goal of many prominent mathematicians. In the late 16th century a German mathematician, van Ceulen, calculated π to 36 decimal places and requested that this value be inscribed on his tombstone. In 1824 its value was calculated by Gauss to 200 places and in 1854 by Shanks to 707 places, after 10 000 hours of endeavour.

This lesson begins with a revision of the concept of π and an introduction to the concept of radian measure. From this foundation MATHOMAT shapes are used to construct diagrams that demonstrate the relationship between the unit circle and the number line on which the circle is 'unwrapped'. From here the definition of the sine of an angle follows and the graph is drawn as a natural consequence.

Before the lesson begins make overhead transparencies of the seven diagrams provided in Transparencies 11.1, 11.2 and 11.3. Diagram 1 on Transparency 11.1 includes a face. Cut this from the transparency for use as an independent entity—it will be used to illustrate key aspects of a ride on a ferris wheel.

A toy ferris wheel is a useful discussion aid—ask interested students to make one from a construction kit before the lesson.

A number of sessions will be required to complete all of the activities in this lesson.

Lesson Outline

1. Estimating the value of π

Although most students can recite the deceptively simple formula C=2πr, a thorough understanding of what it and its components really mean is necessary before using the unit circle to introduce trigonometric functions.

Initial discussions and demonstrations with real circles (bike wheels, cans) should establish that π is a number 'a bit bigger than 3'—the activities to achieve this are described in the following paragraphs.

This part of the lesson works best if students are organised into groups of five or six.

Ask each group to measure the radius and circumference of each of a number of circular objects, enter their measurements into Worksheet 11.1, Estimating π, and calculate the ratio C/2r, using a calculator or spreadsheet.

Circular object	Circumference, C	Radius, r	C/2π
Plate			
Jam jar			
Bike wheel			
Trundle wheel			

An efficient method of measuring circumferences is by wrapping string around the circular objects; another is by rolling the objects for exactly one revolution on a flat surface. Since each of these methods relates directly to concepts developed later in the lesson, students should experience them both.

Use class discussion to compare different groups' methods and their results. A final value of π should be agreed upon—this might be the mean of all calculated values.

As a closing activity for this part of the lesson, ask students to graphically summarise the information in their tables by plotting C (vertical axis) against r (horizontal axis) and discuss the outcome.

Present a brief account of the history of π and its value (3.14159265) to several decimal places.

2. Measuring distances around the unit circle

Introduce the idea of a point moving around the circumference of a circle using the model of a person's ride on a ferris wheel. Use the transparencies of the ferris wheel and the face, together with coloured pens, to illustrate key aspects of the person's ride as mentioned in the next paragraph. A toy ferris wheel would also aid discussion.

At any instant the person's height above or below the axis can be estimated and the person's journey should be discussed in terms of height, the distance travelled along the circumference and its repetitive aspects. For example: how far has the person travelled in moving from A to B; from A to C; from A to D; from A to A?

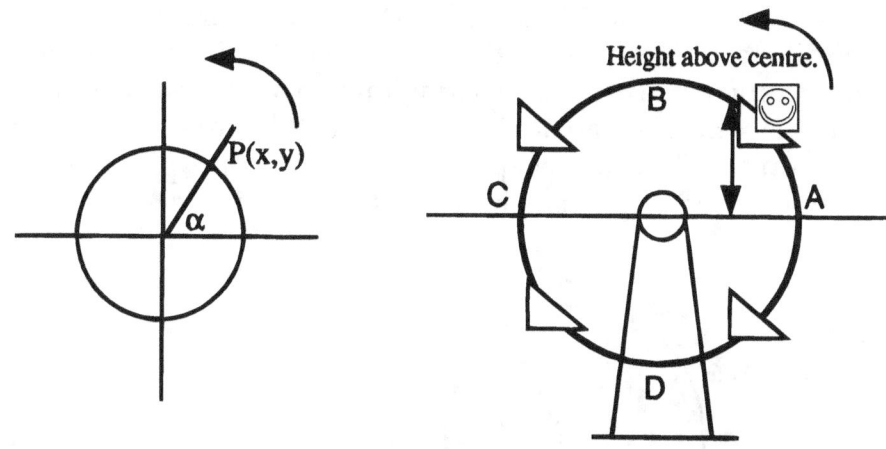

Revise the concept of the angle of rotation, conventionally measured anti-clockwise from the positive x axis, in terms of the person's ride on the ferris wheel. For example: what is the angle from A to D; what is the angle of each of the four seats on the wheel in the diagram? Now guide discussion from the ferris wheel to a similar discussion of a point moving around a unit circle. Emphasise that if the radius of a circle is 1 then the length of the circumference is 2π, the length of the semi-circle is π, the length of the arc of a quarter of the circle is $\pi/2$ etc. The diagram below (Diagram 4, Transparency 11.2)
summarises significant distances around the circumference of the unit circle. In the next part of the lesson students produce copies of this diagram.

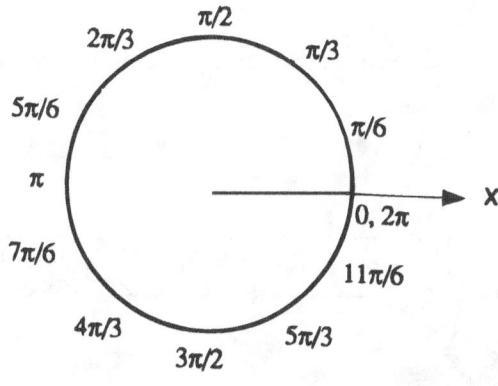

3. Using radians to measure angles

The idea of the radian being another way of measuring angles is introduced in this section.

Use Diagram 3, Transparency 11.2, to show that a string wrapped around part of the circumference of a unit circle subtends an angle at the centre of the circle.

Explain that if the length of the string is equal to the radius of the circle then the angle is, by definition, one radian. Extend this to 'other pieces of string': if the string has length $\pi/2$ (a quarter of the circumference) then the angle is $\pi/2$ radian and similarly for each of the 'string lengths' marked on the circle below (Diagram 5, Transparency 11.2).

Ask students to use MATHOMAT shape 3 to draw a unit circle and accurately reproduce the diagram below: emphasise that each of the 12 evenly spaced points on the circumference has associated with it an arc whose length is measured from the x-axis, and an angle subtended at the centre of the circle. (Each gradation on MATHOMAT shape 3 is 6°. (See Lesson 7, part 4, for further discussion of dividing circles into equal parts.)

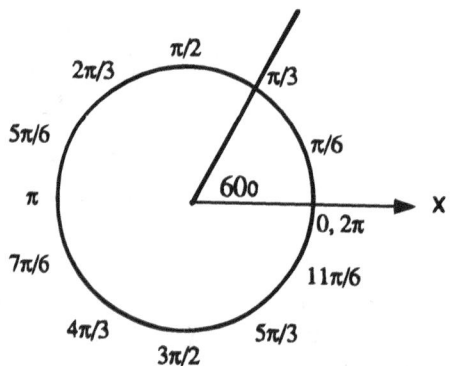

Ask students to calculate the angles associated with each point marked on the circumference of the circle and use these to complete the second and third columns of the table in Worksheet 11.2, Measuring the Sines of Angles.

4. Using the MATHOMAT to produce an 'unwrapped' circle

MATHOMAT shape 3 is designed to be used as a unit circle in association with the linear radian scale which is on the bottom edge of the MATHOMAT. The diagram below shows how one unit on this scale is equal to the radius of the unit circle, shape 3.

The radius of the circle is the unit of the linear scale.

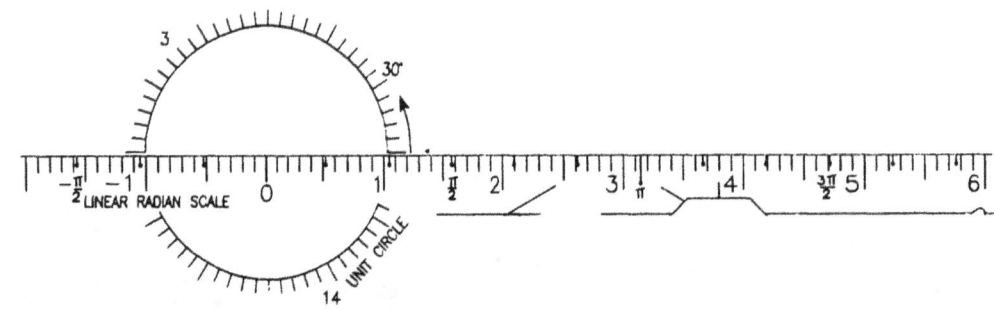

Students must understand the relationship between these components of the MATHOMAT if they are to use them in the remainder of the lesson.

Discuss with students the fact that integer units on the linear scale are labelled, as are the positions of $-\pi$, $-\pi/2$, $\pi/2$, π, $3\pi/2$ and 2π. Indicate that if the circumference were to be 'unwrapped' and laid along the linear scale then correspondingly labelled points would exactly match.

Also marked on the linear scale, but not explicitly labelled, are points that are multiples of $\pi/6$. Identify these as they allow a direct mapping of the circle onto the scale.

Ask students to use MATHOMAT shape 3 and the linear radian scale to produce their own accurate copy of the following diagram—they will use their copies of this diagram in part 7 of the lesson.

Multiples of π on the unit circle and on the corresponding linear scale

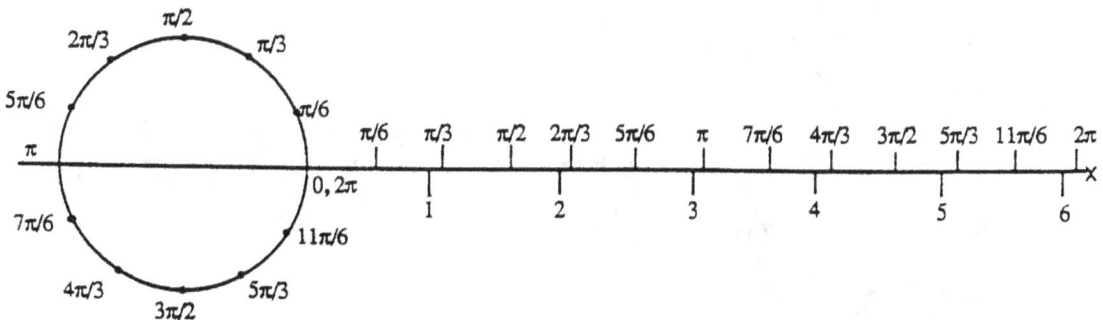

Two important points to emphasise in discussion are that:

- the linear radian scale is a number line with labels for fractions of π as well as the integers; and

- the unit length on the linear scale is equal to the radius of the circle, and therefore the scale can be considered an 'unwrapping' of the circle.

5. Defining the sine of an angle

Corresponding to every point P(x,y) on the unit circle there is an angle α.

Point P(x,y) on the unit circle and the corresponding angle α

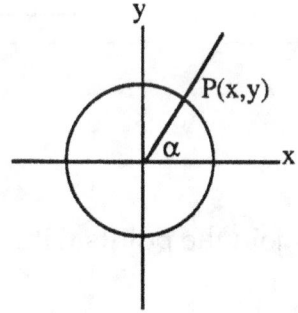

The sine of the angle α is defined as y, the height of P above the x-axis.
So, by definition:

$$\sin \alpha = y.$$

Illustrate how 'y' varies by selecting, on the transparency of the ferris wheel or the unit circle, a variety of angles in the range 0° to 360°. Do not give precise numerical values at this stage; however, the increasing and decreasing nature of y and its minimum and maximum values and periodicity should be discussed.

6. Drawing the sine graph

The following diagram illustrates how to plot points for the sine graph. The point shown is obtained as the intersection of the line drawn vertically from π/3 on the x-axis with the line drawn horizontally from π/3 on the unit circle.

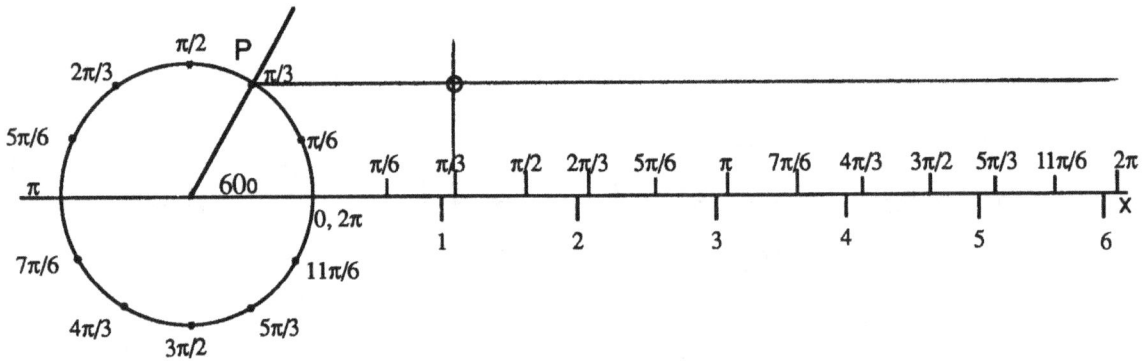

Ask students to use the MATHOMAT to draw additional horizontal lines on the diagrams of the 'unwrapped' circles they produced in part 4 of this lesson, and then plot points corresponding to the sines of each of the angles marked on the rim of the circle.

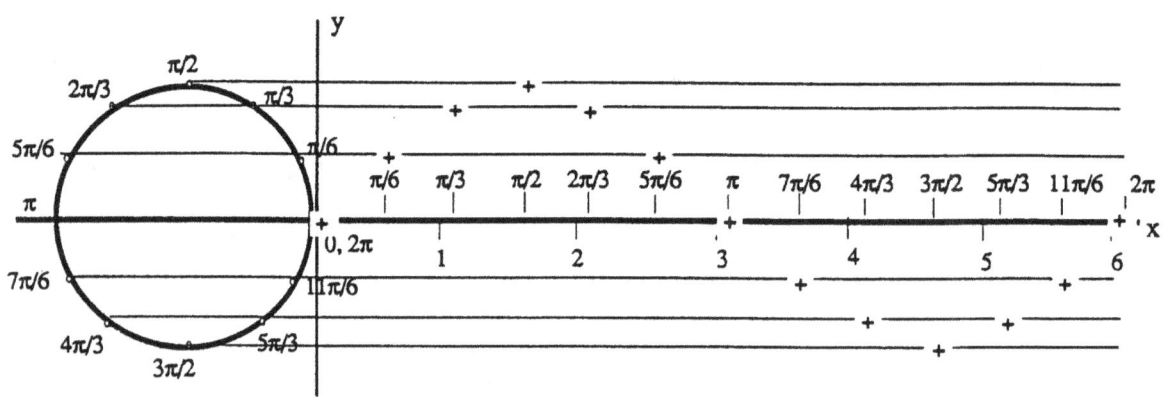

Ask the students to carefully join the points with a smooth curve to obtain a sine graph.

7. Estimating the sines of angles

To obtain a numerical estimate of the sine of an angle, the angle can be drawn onto the unit circle and 'y' measured directly with the MATHOMAT linear scale.

As a final activity, ask students to obtain numerical estimates for the sines of each of the angles in the table in Worksheet 11.2, Measuring the Sines of Angles, and record these in column 4 of the table. They can compare these values with those obtained from their calculators, which they enter into the fifth column of the table.

Estimating π

Circular object	Circumference, C	Radius, r	$C/2\pi$
Plate			
Jam jar			
Bike wheel			
Trundle wheel			

Measuring the Sines of Angles

Distance round circle	Angle		Sine of angle	
	degrees	radians	measured	calculator
0				
$\pi/6$				
$\pi/3$				
$\pi/2$				
$2\pi/3$				
$5\pi/6$				
π				
$7\pi/6$				
$4\pi/3$				
$3\pi/2$				
$5\pi/3$				
$11\pi/6$				
2π				

Unwrapping the Circle
Diagrams 1 and 2

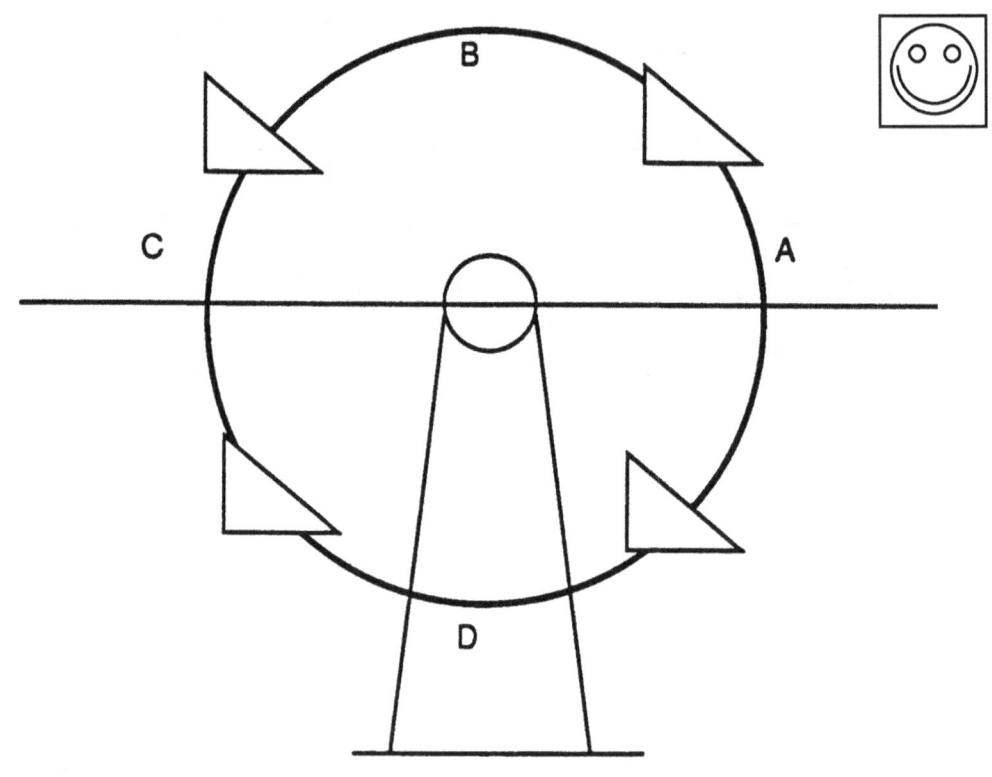

Diagram 1

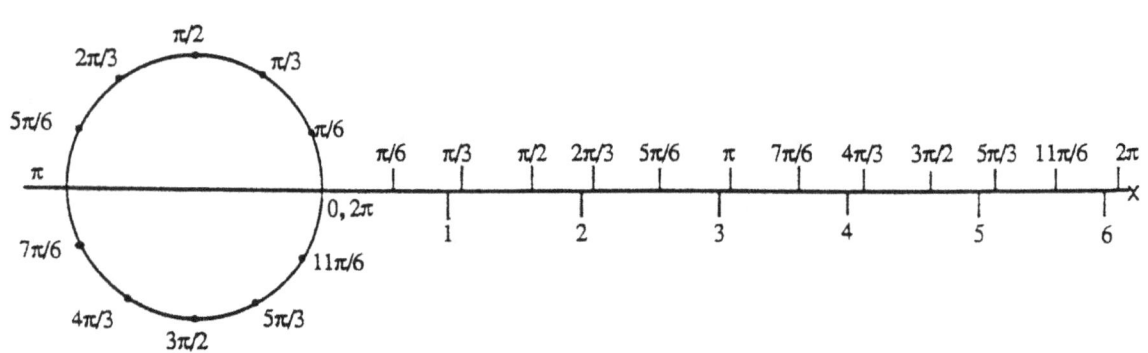

Unwrapping the Circle
Diagrams 3, 4 and 5

Diagram 3

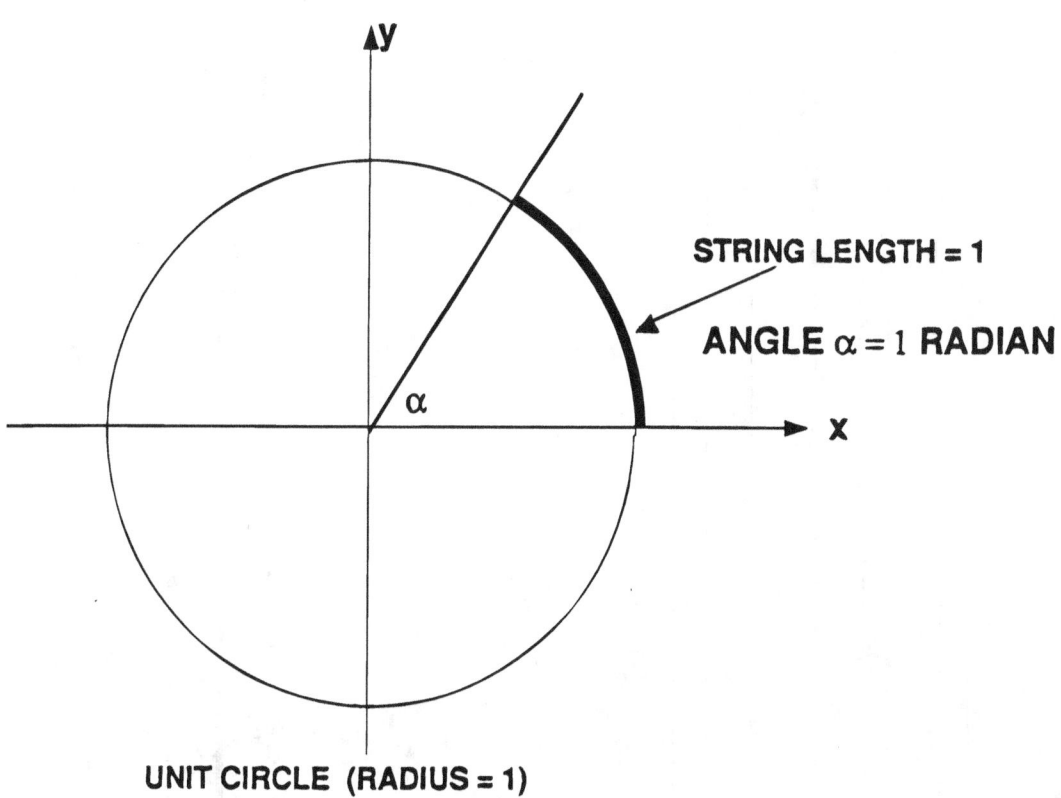

Diagram 4

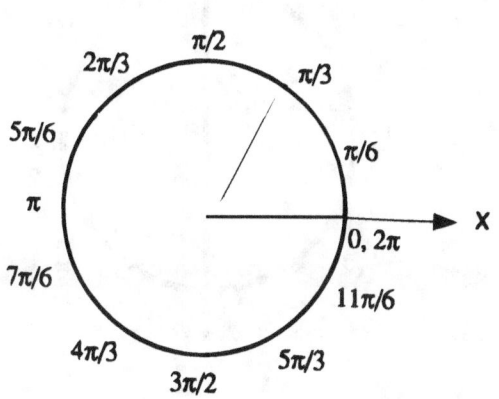

Diagram 5

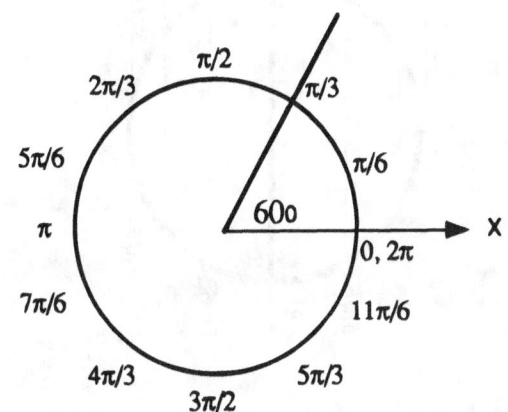

Unwrapping the Circle
Diagrams 6 and 7

Diagram 6

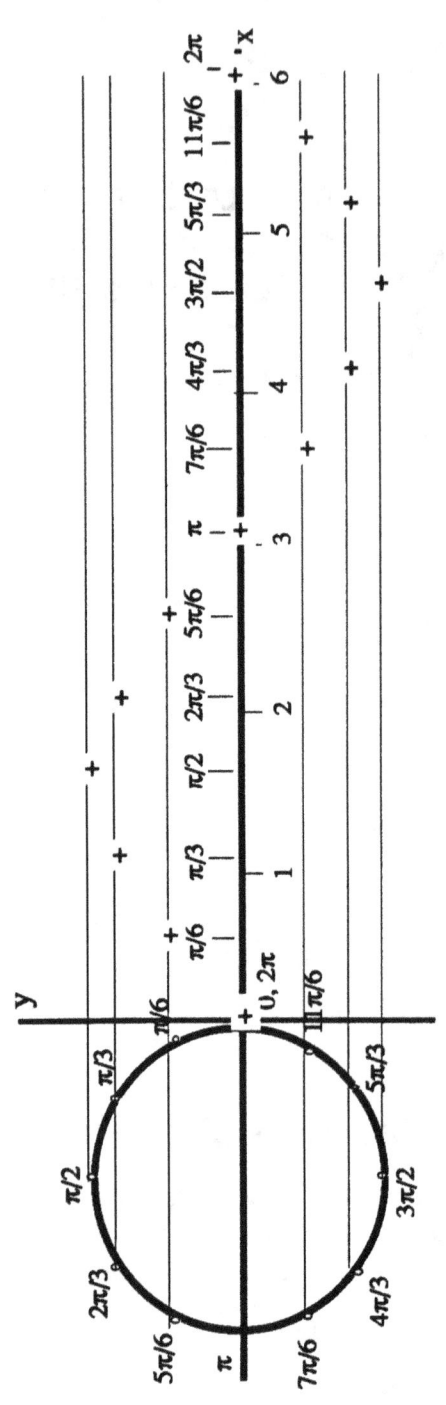

Diagram 7

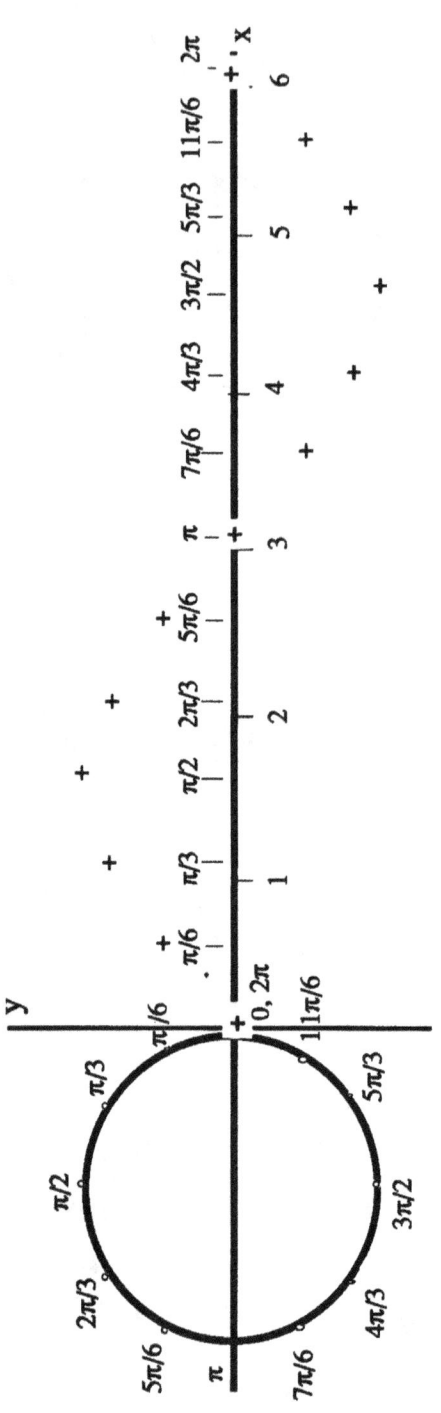

www.ingramcontent.com/pod-product-compliance
Lightning Source LLC
Chambersburg PA
CBHW080834010526

44112CB00016B/2510